The foe claims in error that a philosopher I am.
God knows I am not what he says I am.
But, having endured this sorrow's nest, I ask:
Why should I not know at least what I am?

—Omar Khayyam

HUMAN ARCHITECTURE

Journal of the Sociology of Self-Knowledge

Editor:

Mohammad H. (Behrooz) Tamdgidi
Associate Professor of Sociology
UMass Boston

Human Architecture: Journal of the Sociology of Self-Knowledge (ISSN # 1540-5699) is published by OKCIR: the Omar Khayyam Center for Integrative Research in Utopia, Mysticism, and Science (www.okcir.com, info@okcir.com) and printed by the Okcir Press, an imprint of Ahead Publishing House (APH), P. O. Box 393, Belmont, MA, 02478, U.S.A., tel/fax: 617.932.1170. Copyright © by Ahead Publishing House, 2002-9. All rights reserved. *Human Architecture* is indexed in CSA Illumina's *Sociological Abstracts*® and complied in EBSCO's SocINDEX with Full-Text® and ProQuest's "Social Science Journals" full-text database.

Submissions: *Human Architecture* publishes both submitted and invited manuscripts as well as the working papers of OKCIR: the Omar Khayyam Center for Integrative Research in Utopia, Mysticism, and Science—an independent research and educational project. Contributors extend permission to *Human Architecture* for the publication of their work in the journal. They retain copyrights to their work and may publish them elsewhere. If the submitted manuscript has been published elsewhere before, written permission from both the author(s) and publication(s) where it earlier appeared should accompany submission to *Human Architecture*.

Editorial decisions: *Human Architecture* adheres to the peer reviewing principle for advancing scholarship—seeking innovative ways to meet the need in favor of liberatory scholarly practices most conducive to the aim and purpose of the journal. Selection of papers from submitted or invited manuscripts are based on their substantive relevance and the coherence and innovativeness of their argument in consideration of the mission of the journal. Views expressed in the journal by contributors are those of their authors and may not necessarily coincide with one another, or with the views of the editor, members of the Editorial Advisory Board, or the institutions with which any of the above are affiliated. Authors are solely responsible for the accuracy and integrity of factual, bibliographic, and referential materials used in their own articles, and for obtaining permissions for using copyrighted material in their manuscripts. Methodological, theoretical, historical, empirical, practical, as well as literary and artistic contributions relevant to the mission of the journal are all encouraged. The primary language used is English, but material in other languages may be included if relevant to the purpose of the journal.

What to submit: All manuscripts should be submitted in electronic format. They should preferably be double-spaced in Times 12 typeface., with 1 inch margins all around. Footnotes, endnotes, or reference lists may be single-spaced. In general, authors should follow a consistent bibliographic and citation style of their choice throughout the manuscript. Using the ASA (American Sociological Association) style is preferred by the editor.

Where to submit: The Editor, *Human Architecture*, Okcir Press, P. O. Box 393, Belmont, MA, 02478, U.S.A., tel/fax: 617.932.1170, e-mail: mohammad.tamdgidi@umb.edu

Subscriptions: *Human Architecture* is a quarterly publication, published in either single-issue or double-issue formats, all issues for each volume becoming usually available concurrently at the end of every summer. Individual and institutional rates are $15 and $30 for single-issues and $30 and $60 for double-issues respectively. *Individual and institutional subscription rates* per year beginning from the most recently published issue (when subscription order is received) are $60 and $120 respectively. Back issues or additional copies of the journal are available upon request at the same rates as indicated above. Rates include domestic shipping and sales tax, where applicable. For international or bulk orders please inquire for special rates & shipping charges. Make checks payable in U.S. dollars to Ahead Publishing House, and send payments to Ahead Publishing House, P. O. Box 393, Belmont, MA, 02478, U.S.A. Contributors each receive one free copy of the issue in which their articles appear. Rates are subjected to change without notice.

Advertisements: Current rates and specifications may be obtained by contacting the Okcir Press, P. O. Box 393, Belmont, MA, 02478, U.S.A., tel/fax: 617.932.1170, e-mail: mohammad.tamdgidi@umb.edu

Inquiries: Address all correspondence and requests to *Human Architecture*, Okcir Press, P. O. Box 393, Belmont, MA, 02478, U.S.A., tel/fax: 617.932.1170, e-mail: mohammad.tamdgidi@umb.edu

Changes of address: Six weeks' advance notice must be given when notifying change of address. Please include both the old and the new addresses in your request. **Postmaster:** Send address changes to Ahead Publishing House, P. O. Box 393, Belmont, MA, 02478, U.S.A.

ISBN 978-1-888024-36-4
90000>

9 781888 024364

Human Architecture:
Journal of the Sociology of Self-Knowledge
Volume VII, Special Issue, 2009
ISSN: 1540-5699
ISBN: 978-1-888024-36-4

A Peer-Review*ing* Journal

Contributions to *Human Architecture: Journal of the Sociology of Self-Knowledge* pass through a rigorous selective process with respect to their fit, relevance, coherence of argument, and innovativeness in consideration of the scope, nature, and intended purpose of the journal. The journal adheres to the peer-reviewing principle for advancing scholarship, but aims to design and build new scholarly avenues to meet this requirement—seeking mechanisms that foster openness of inquiry and evaluation; mechanisms that invite constructive judgments subject to free, open, and mutually interactive, not blinded and one-sided, peer reviewing practices; mechanisms that can be employed as widely and dynamically as possible among specialist and interested scholars in the field who value the need for the proliferation of new, critical, and innovative personal and global insights and transformations.

To meet the highest standards of scholarship, liberatory editorial practices need to transition from static peer review*ed* to dynamic peer review*ing* models that de-couple publication from defective pre-publication peer review requirements, and engage in alternative peer review practices that remain open to all those wishing to review a manuscript at any time in the post-publication phase—encouraging expanded and deepening exchanges among scholars, authors and readers alike. They need to invite critical thinking about prevailing and dominant paradigms and inflame creative spirits to forge new scholarly horizons and intellectual landscapes. And they need to embrace the subaltern voices in the academia and beyond, voices of those who have been deprived of cultivating their sociological imaginations through formal scholarly publishing avenues.

Human Architecture warmly invites contributors and readers to peer review the articles herein and to openly share their critical and constructive insights with one another in the future chronicles of this journal.

Contents

HUMAN ARCHITECTURE
Journal of the Sociology of Self-Knowledge

Volume VII   Special Issue   2009

Contents

HUMAN ARCHITECTURE
Journal of the Sociology of Self-Knowledge

Volume VII   Special Issue   2009

Editor's Note: Mahmoud Darwish's Parting Gift

Mohammad H. Tamdgidi

University of Massachusetts Boston

mohammad.tamdgidi@umb.edu

Abstract: This is an editor's note to the Special 2009 issue of *Human Architecture: Journal of the Sociology of Self-Knowledge* in commemoration of Mahmoud Darwish (1941-2008), the Palestinian National Poet. The issue is titled "If I touch the depths of your heart…": The Human Promise of Poetry in Memories of Mahmoud Darwish." Besides providing an overview and appreciation of the contributions in the volume, the editor notes: "The basic gift that I personally take out of publishing this special issue and its considerable peer reviewing experience, one that I call Darwish's parting gift to me, co-editors and contributors in this volume, I think, is that poetry is not just about writing, but also about reading it, about the art of listening as well, to be able to reach out and let the message touch one's heart. The Palestinian challenge and cause, in their essence, is about not only telling, but also listening to oneself and to the other. That, it seems to me, is the lesson I am taking from this experience, thanks to all the considerable efforts made by all the co-editors and the voices of all the contributors."

I long for my mother's bread
My mother's coffee
Her touch
Childhood memories grow up in me
Day after day
I must be worth my life
At the hour of my death
Worth the tears of my mother

And if I come back one day
Take me as a veil to your eyelashes
Cover my bones with the grass
Blessed by your footsteps

Bind us together
with a lock of your hair
With a thread that trails from the back of your
* dress*
I might become immortal
Become a god
If I touch the depths of your heart

If I come back
Use me as wood to feed your fire
As the clothesline on the roof of your house
Without your blessing
I am too weak to stand

Mohammad H. Tamdgidi is Associate Professor of Sociology, teaching social theory at the University of Massachusetts Boston. Most recently he has authored *Gurdjieff and Hypnosis: A Hermeneutic Study* (Palgrave Macmillan, forthcoming/2009), and *Advancing Utopistics: The Three Component Parts and Errors of Marxism* (2007, paperback edition 2009) and is founding editor of *Human Architecture: Journal of the Sociology of Self-Knowledge*, a publication of OKCIR: The Omar Khayyam Center for Integrative Research in Utopia, Mysticism, and Science (Utopystics) which serves to frame his research, teaching, and professional initiatives. Tamdgidi has edited various collections on Paulo Freire, Edward Said, Gloria Anzaldúa, Frantz Fanon, and Thich Nhat Hanh, and his writings have appeared in *Sociological Spectrum*, *Review* (Journal of the Fernand Braudel Center for the Study of Economies, Historical Systems, and Civilizations), *Humanity & Society, Contemporary Sociology*, and several other edited volumes.

I am old
Give me back the star maps of childhood
So that I
Along with the Swallows
Can chart the path
Back to your waiting nest
                    —Mahmoud Darwish,
          "I Long for My Mother's Bread"

Mahmoud Darwish (1941-2008), one of the greatest contemporary Arab and world poets, was born in Palestine. His family fled in 1948 when Israeli forces attacked his village. He lived in Israel and Lebanon, studied in Moscow and worked in Paris as editor-in-chief of the literary journal *Al-Karmel*. He published more than thirty volumes of poetry and eight books of prose and was regarded as Palestine's Poet Laureate.

"I thought poetry could change everything, could change history and could humanize," Darwish said in an interview with *The Progressive* in 2002, "and I think that the illusion is very necessary to push poets to be involved and to believe... but now I think that poetry changes only the poet" (http://www.progressive.org/node/1575; article by Nathalie Handal). Yet, it is not difficult to find millions around the world who have been deeply touched at heart by the power and promise of his poetry. *Common Ground News* featured a mourning for Darwish on August 14, 2008, where his words, "I had enough yesterdays; what I need is a tomorrow" are remembered. Recalled also are the following words expressed by Darwish during his last performance in July 2008 in Ramallah, words that convey the depth of Darwish's heart and the sociological imagination inspiring his poetry:

As you prepare your breakfast—think of others. Don't forget to feed the pigeons. As you conduct your wars—think of others. Don't forget those who want peace. As you pay your water bill—think of others. Think of those who only have clouds to drink from. As you go home, your own home—think of others—don't forget those who live in tents. As you sleep and count the planets, think of others—there are people who have no place to sleep. As you liberate yourself with metaphors think of others—those who have lost their right to speak. And as you think of distant others—think of yourself and say "I wish I were a candle in the darkness." (http://www.commongroundnews.org/article.php?id=23736&lan=en&sid=0&sp=0; translated and included in the article by Ibtisam Barakat)

This special 2009 issue of *Human Architecture: Journal of the Sociology of Self-Knowledge* is dedicated to the theme "If I touch the depths of your heart": The Human Promise of Poetry in Memories of Mahmoud Darwish." A collective of dedicated co-editors at UMass Boston comprised of (alphabetically) Anna D. Beckwith (Sociology), Elora Chowdhury (Women's Studies), Leila Farsakh (Political Science), Askold Melnyczuk (English), Erica Mena (UMass Boston Alumni), Dorothy Nelson (English), Joyce Peseroff (English), and Rajini Srikanth (English), dedicated much of their time, love, and attention to realizing this special issue in collaboration with the journal editor as a parting gift from Mahmoud Darwish—a gift not only to readers, but also a gift to one another, of keeping a wonderful and engaging conversation with one another for many months. My thanks to them all for their generous words, thoughts, understandings, and energies. The beautiful expression "human promise of poetry" was one used as the title of an event at UMass Boston in late Fall 2008 (December 9, 2009) organized by Dorothy Shubow Nelson, Rajini Srikanth, Leila Farsakh, Askold Melnyczuk, Joyce Peseroff, Erica Mena, and others to belatedly commemorate the untimely passing of Mahmoud Darwish on March 3, 2008 and to remember and recite his life and poetry amid a wide campus audience. My proposal later to devote an issue of *Human Architecture* to Mahmoud Darwish may have been delayed if it was not for the warm and heart-felt encouragement of Dorothy Shubow Nelson who in later months became a most dedicated and engaged co-editor alongside other colleagues.

We were enormously pleased and fortunate to receive a series of wonderful submissions from many voices that adorn the pages of this special issue on Darwish, a fact that speaks to the power of Darwish's life (and passing) to touch the depths of the hearts of so many around the world throughout the decades. Other than keynote opening statements, the special issue is comprised of a selected series of longer and shorter poems by Mahmoud Darwish, followed by commemorative poetry, and then commemorative essays/articles that directly or indirectly engage with Mahmoud Darwish's work and/or the subject matter of his passion and love, Palestine and human rights and dignity.

UMass Boston Provost and Vice Chancellor for Academic Affairs, Winston Langley, generously continued his by now relatively long tradition of contributing an opening key statement to the journal, in this case titled "Candle," having read almost all of the contributions before drafting his moving statement. Martha Collins shared with us her stunningly moving and expressive words in "For Gaza," ones that resonate well in the hearts and minds of all those who witnessed through the media and news the tragedies of Gaza in the ending days of 2008 and early days of 2009. She had recited her poem in an event on January 30, 2009, in Cambridge, MA, protesting the atrocities being committed in Gaza. It is thanks to co-editor Askold Melnyczuk who invited her (and Robert Lipton, see further below) to contribute to the issue, that we

can share the gift, in memory of Mahmoud Darwish, of her poem.

We are deeply appreciative of Palestinian-American poet and major translator of Mahmoud Darwish's work, Fady Joudah, who contacted the editors for consideration of sharing his introduction to a still-yet-to-be-finalized/published collection of translations of Darwish's poetry, titled *If I Were Another: Poems* (Farrar, Straus and Giroux, 2009). We are grateful to him, and to Joyce Peseroff who reminded me again later in the process to contact Joudah to inquire into the possibility. He graciously offered the introduction from his forthcoming book, and facilitated not only the acquiring of permission from the publisher, but also proposed the publication of selections from Darwish's shorter poems from *A River Dies of Thirst: Journals*, as masterly translated from the Arabic by Catherine Cobham. Again Joudah offered the necessary contacts to acquire the necessary permissions from the latter collection's publisher, Archipelago, NY. The representation of Darwish's voice in the collection, in the form of three longer poems ("The 'Red Indian's' Penultimate Speech to the White Man"; "Tuesday and the Weather is Clear"; and "Hoopoe"), and seven shorter ones ("A River Dies of Thirst"; "Assassination"; "Nero"; "The Enemy"; "The House as Casualty"; "The Rest of A Life"; and "If We Want To"), then is owed to Fady Joudah (and by extension Catherine Cobham) and their publishers and we are very thankful of that. I strongly urge readers to seek the new latest collections of Darwish's poetry as noted above.

Then we are most fortunate to have a collection of gifts of poetry from Lisa Suhair Majaj, another major Palestinian-American poet, writer and scholar. Her keynote poems are very moving and most representative of the inspiring offerings that, as in Darwish, come to us from the struggles and toils of Palestinians. Amy Tighe's letter to Darwish speaks to the very heart of our call for papers/submissions for the issue, for through her poem/letter she speaks so eloquently and clearly why Darwish's humble words that poet only changes him/herself and not the world needs second thinking. Dorothy Shubow Nelson's poem "Truth" speaks to the hopes and pains of the separated families of Jews and Palestinians in search of a lasting peace and return to their common peoplehood, while Joyce Peseroff's poem "American Idol" invites us to seriously reflect on the changing (or not) nature of warfare, such as those waged by Israel in Gaza, through the millennia. Robert Lipton, in "Darwish Sits In" weaves the everyday moments and the larger historical predicament of Palestinians as conveyed through the poetic sense of Mahmoud Darwish, while Fady Joudah, who also kindly offered one of his own poems for the collection, titled "Wreck," directs our attention, in his own words, to the fact that "so much of the architecture of contemporary humanitarianism gives over the role of master morality at the expense of a true affirmation of life."

Shaari Neretin, invited to contribute by co-editor and Palestinian scholar Leila Farsakh, provides a compelling sense, in the form of a metaphor "The Lost and Found Warehouse" for what it must be like for a whole people to be faced with the loss of one's not only land and lives, but also with that of one's memories, while poet Jack Hirschman, memorializes Mahmoud Darwish, in his poem "Mantra for Mahmoud Darwish" offered in French and kindly translated by co-editor Erica Mena.

Then we have a series of excellent essays and articles in commemoration of Darwish, his work, and the historical context that embraced him. Leila Farsakh's keynote essay gives flesh and blood to the minute everyday ways in which Palestinians enjoyed and were moved and inspired by Darwish's poetry throughout decades. Rajini Srikanth shares with her readers, as frankly as it is courageous, her growing up challenges of learning about the Palestinian

people's struggles, and in doing so, practices a sociological imagination exemplary for many sociologists to follow. Erica Mena makes significant contribution to understanding a dimension of Darwish's life and work that may perhaps be lost in the attention given to his immediate struggles for Palestinian rights to national self-determination; Mena directs our attention to the paradoxical consideration that what made Darwish and his work so influential worldwide was his ability to speak not only critically about his people's immediate tasks, but also the broader post-national sensibilities, historically long-delayed, that Darwish also speaks to and promote through his poetry.

Kyleen Aldrich presents an important voice in comparing the historical dilemmas facing Palestinians and Native Americans, through her comparative analysis of the works of Darwish and Silko, while Nadia Alahmed pursues a similar aim, by creatively comparing the struggles of Palestinians and African-Americans as framed by the matrix of nationalism. And finally, Patrick Sylvain, extends an in-depth analysis of Darwish's work and poetry in both historical and biographical contexts.

The basic gift that I personally take out of publishing this special issue, one that I call Darwish's parting gift to us, co-editors and contributors in this volume, I think, is that poetry is not just about writing, but also about reading it, about the art of listening as well, to be able to reach out and let the message touch one's heart. The Palestinian challenge and cause, in their essence, is about not only telling, but also listening to oneself and to the other. That, it seems to me, is the lesson I am taking from this experience, thanks to all the considerable efforts made by all the co-editors and the voices of all the contributors.

Just to give the reader a taste of conversation that accompanied the significant and serious peer reviewing and publication of this issue, I can cite a few examples from the contributions of the co-editor Dorothy Shubow Nelson:

Dear Behrooz, I have just finished reading Nadia Alahmed's comparative paper (26 pages) on the Black Arts Movement and the Palestinian Culture of Resistance. I was thrilled to read this fascinating paper and experience the energetic commitment of Nadia Alahmed to this project. In addition to describing the historical and political roots of these movements her paper shows how the cultural works that emerged "erased the borders" between politics and art. Poetry, because of its moral vision, passion and hope, can help to create the country. Scholars and writers are integrated fluently throughout these pages and contribute to making the historical moments which created the momentum for these artistic movements, come alive. … When the poems begin to appear on these pages (Darwish's poetry as well as others) with critical commentary, the reader is riveted. The recognizing powers of the mind are fused with and illuminated and heightened by the imagination. There is so much to learn from reading this paper.

Alahmed informs us that "Traces of Darwish's poetry can be found on the political documents of the P.L.O," for example. As well, there are important reasons to revisit the origins and development of the Black Arts movements of the 60's and 70's. The essay is liberationist throughout: for example, revolutionary leaders and forces that influenced the political development of many in the Black Arts Movement are acknowledged. In addition the "neo-colonial nature of the state of Israel" is discussed directly and forcefully. Alahmed's explication of Fanon's theory of culture in

oppressed countries is a springboard for her astute comparisons. She asserts that "culture is one of the main targets of the oppressors"… and "Culture gives us a revolutionary moral vision and a system of values and a methodology around which to shape the political movement." Reading this paper confirms and deepens our understanding of the love for and continued devotion to Mahmoud Darwish. Sincerely, Dorothy.

Regarding Fady Joudah's translations of Darwish's poetry in *If I Were Another: Poems*, Nelson had the following to offer:

I have just finished reading the first 100 pages of IF I WERE ANOTHER and wanted to share my thoughts briefly with you. …

This is a challenging task—to choose a few poems from this extraordinary collection of Darwish's work. From the first poem to the one I just finished (A Horse for the Stranger) I was carried away, completely absorbed and taken in by the language, tone, lines, cadences, historic scope, ironies, electric metaphoric expressions and the determination of the poet to reach for what is almost inexpressible in these poems. The poems soar like the birds that Darwish speaks of. The connection of human existences to the earth and all living things is both ancient and very contemporary here. I felt the presence of the poet and the emotional power of the poems strongly as I have in reading *Memory for Forgetfulness* which was translated by Ibrahim Muhawi. Darwish's reading of ancient scriptures (Arabic and Hebrew) bring these poetic texts to life. In A Horse for the Stranger, The West is awakened to an Iraq that is not the Iraq they know.

I appreciate so much Nelson's and all issue co-editors for the gift of conversations on this journal issues.

As editor of this issue, I must say that working on it has encouraged me to be even more than usual open, to listen, and to try to understand the other; and this I consider to be Darwish's parting gift to me personally. Perhaps a poem's touching one's heart is a two-way street, and not just a result of efforts and skill of the master poet. And it is this insight, perhaps, that may explain why poems can change life. Perhaps the answer to Darwish's question, regarding whether poem can change the world or not, is somewhere in between, and not predetermined. Poetry CAN change both the poet and the world. It may not change one or the other, but it CAN, and this requires the participation of both the poet and the reader. And as Amy Tighe, the listener to Darwish's voice, writes by example in her letter to Darwish, listening to poems is and must be seen as an integral part of its art. So, we have many further poets in you, the reader, to reach out to, by publishing this issue, and having you read it.

One last, final point, is in order before I close this already long editor's note. This relates to the journal's cover image. I was struck by the image, when it first emerged soon after the Israeli invasion of Gaza in Dec. 2008-January 2009. The image is quite powerful, and speaks to the depth of strength, hope, energy and inspiration of Palestine and its people. Amid such tragedy and horror, its children express their humanity and love for life, and the continuity of their struggles, so well, simply, and powerfully. A living poem indeed, a Darwish resurrecting from the rubble, his wood firing the hope of those witnessing the children's play.

Meanwhile, I was shocked and deeply saddened by the images coming from Iran recently, specially the bullet piercing the heart of Neda Agha Soltan, who was so innocently killed just for expressing her wish that her vote be counted. There have been many others killed, injured, and yes, over many decades, on all sides of the Iranian social conflict as well. Tragedies have befallen Iran too, and it has had its own shares and forms of them. The look of imminent death in the rolling eyes of Neda just before her sudden passing has haunted me as so many others, and reminded me so painfully of the look in the eyes of the Palestinian boy Mohammed just before he died a few years ago being protected by his father against the bullets of Israeli soldiers amid a cross fire. The look in the eyes were exactly the same, the horror of the moment was captured by the sophisticated technologies, which were not invented for transformative purposes, but for "American Idol" (see Joyce Peseroff's poem in this issue) entertainments, perhaps. But people are inventive, creative, and make new uses of the "Antikythera mechanisms" of today in exposing the modern achilles' war conquests. But amid the deepening conflict in Iran, and in a global context as well, what the image of the children of Gaza on the journal cover conveys is strength and hope, of joy amid adversity, and of coping with hardships amid a long, long struggle. Iranians can again learn a lesson or two from the hopeful and skin-thick children of Gaza, in whose veins and skeletons and flesh and blood, Darwish and his spirit is living. On their makeshift razed playground they tell us not to give up hope in making sure their lives, and votes, are counted.

In a last communication from Lisa Suhair Majaj, she wrote:

> "Ah, if only Mahmoud Darwish were here to see our humble honoring of him!"

I can't find a better way to end this editor's note, and on behalf of all the issue co-editors, and let the reader move on to the heart of the human promise of poetry in the following memories of Mahmoud Darwish.

The Candle

Winston Langley

University of Massachusetts Boston

winston.langley@umb.edu

Abstract: This is a keynote statement by Winston Langley, Provost, Vice Chancellor of Academic Affairs, and Professor of International Relations at UMass Boston, opening the special 2009 issue of *Human Architecture: Journal of the Sociology of Self-Knowledge* dedicated to the memory and poetry of Mahmoud Darwish (1941–2008), the national poet of Palestine. In Provost Langley's view this issue of the journal merits the qualifying expression "special," because of the person it seeks to honor, the grounds that have invited that honor, the included voices of those who have sought to be part of this honoring, and the underlying spirit of the issue—one which is so closely tied to the burden of the honoree, Mahmoud Darwish. Provost Langley concludes that no one can read the poetry in this issue—those of Darwish and the contributors—without being moved—and moved to envision a tomorrow, toward which Darwish always looked. He wished he were a candle, in the darkness. He was and will be—for the Palestinians and all those who seek or espouse the cause of human dignity.

This issue of the journal merits the qualifying expression "special," because of the person it seeks to honor, the grounds that have invited that honor, the included voices of those who have sought to be part of this honoring, and the underlying spirit of the issue—one which is so closely tied to the burden of the honoree, Mahmoud Darwish.

Great poets are many things. First, they bring to our senses the genius of place—what it is, how it multiplies, proliferates, in adventures to tell us its stories, how it travels to and through our sights, smells, sounds, images, maxims, beliefs, and how it finds like and likeness. Darwish, uses Palestine, his homeland, as his place of reference, a site of intense toil and travail, of doubt and loss, and of frustration and promise. He uses place to do much more, however, including that of teaching us that the light in which we see orders and regulates seeing. And his urging us to alter our circumstances is, in part, to help us to see and understand the self and other more profoundly.

The great poet, of course, helps to alter some of those circumstances, including the circumstances of our seeing. Despite his doubts respecting the poetry's capacity to effect transformative change, Darwish's work has in fact been ordering the way

Winston Langley is Provost and Vice Chancellor of Academic Affairs, and Professor of Political Science and international Relations at UMass Boston. His interests are in global order and public international law, human rights, alternative models of world order, and religion and politics. He has taught a wide variety of undergraduate and graduate courses including world politics and world order, international political economy, human rights and public policy, and images of world politics in film and literature. Publications include "Nuclear Weapons and the International Court of Justice" in *International Affairs*, and two books, *Women's Rights in the United States: A Documentary History,* and *Human Rights: The Major Global Instruments*. Most recently, Langley is the author of *Kazi Nazrul Islam: The Voice of Poetry and the Struggle for Human Wholeness* (Dhaka: Nazrul Institute, 2007), a book on Nazrul Islam, the national poet of Bangladesh, and his achievements in the area of human rights.

many have come to see Palestine and the world, and it has been transforming many, including other poets, as so clearly demonstrated by contributions to this issue.

This focus on place and on seeing has a bearing on what great poets seek to do in another area—that of finding and exposing the truth of things. In doing so, they do not—as is commonly supposed—pursue "truth for truth's sake," but to serve a major human need for the truth of things, to nurture this much-overlooked feature of the human personality that perhaps most demonstrably distinguishes human beings from non-human animals, and best uncovers, connects, and knits one to our common humanity.

Darwish, as with all great poets, affirms that the life of the mind, of emotions, of living and being, is part of the past (as experienced), the actual present, and the imagined or ideal of human habitats within natural settings of trees, fields, plants, fruits, deserts, seacoasts. The human-made, in the form of houses, streets, friendships, nations, hatreds, beliefs, images—especially as they interact with the natural settings—allows for the broadening of experiences that invite and command naming. Part of a poets calling is to name.

That naming encompasses the struggle against un- or non-belonging, for identity (individual and collective), and on behalf of our broader kinship, or selfsameness, one's human identity. In this struggle for identity, in the face of displacement, alienation, exile, remembering and forgetting, sorrows too deep sometimes to share, we encounter the universal and liberating goal of human striving as a form of development, even in a climate of moral and socio-economic indifference.

Darwish confronts us with all the general themes just mentioned—themes found in language that has been inhabited, made more pliable—line by line—to yield poetry fused with revelatory images—

among which humans move—in feeling, desiring, crying, loving, knowing, supposing, preferring, yearning, suspecting, censoring, and affirming, in embracing and creating beauty, and in claiming their species membership and their dignity. It is to these themes that a group of distinguished contributors responds and does so in compelling form.

These contributors, using essays, comments, poetry (or a combination of all) focus on different aspects of Darwish's work and the Palestinian pursuit of self-determination. Some look at the relationship—as Darwish did—between that pursuit and the struggle of other peoples to be self-determining; some focus on influences on the Palestinian liberation movement; and some look at the West and its implications in that movement. Others explore the linking of cultures and countries, loving disagreement with Darwish, and the struggle for memory. Still others emphasize resistance and compassion, touch on connection between "master morality" and the affirmation of life, or reach for the underlying meaning between Darwish and Palestine. One finds a focus on solidarity with the Palestinians, sisterhood between Jews and Arabs (including Palestinians), hope for both Israel and Palestine, and the ties between intimacy and poetry. Present, as well, are multiple points of emphasis such as the relationship between moments and movements, recognition and action (inaction), and how one may best read Darwish. The latter's poems are generously represented in the volume.

No one can read the poetry in this issue—those of Darwish and the contributors—without being moved—and moved to envision a tomorrow, toward which Darwish always looked. He wished he were a candle, in the darkness. He was and will be—for the Palestinians and all those who seek or espouse the cause of human dignity.

For Gaza

Martha Collins

Poet, Translator, and Editor

martha.collins@oberlin.edu

"For Gaza" by poet Martha Collins belongs to a sequence of poems she wrote in January 2009, when she was reading as much as she could about the siege of Gaza; her sources included the *New York Times, Guardian (UK),* and *New Statesman.* The immediate impetus for this poem was a public reading by political writers and poets in Cambridge, Massachusetts, on January 30, 2009; many of the readings, including her own, featured poems by Mahmoud Darwish. Collins wrote the poem after the gathering, which was itself called "For Gaza."

for the woman who cooks on a fire of sticks and boards beside her shell of a house, her
　　bag of clothes on a tree

for physician Awni al-Jaru, his wife cut in half, his year-old-son *turned to pieces*

for the 30 dead Samouni family members dug out of the rubble, for the living, including
　　children who clutched dead mothers

for the schools and mosques and thousands of homes destroyed by bombs, for the graves
　　disturbed by tanks

for the more than 1300 dead, including those who walked from their homes, as directed,
　　with white flags

for those going home to water their trees, lemon and almond and olive, and for those trees

for Gaza, for Palestine/Israel, for ourselves, for hope for peace

January 30, 2009

Martha Collins is the author of the book-length poem *Blue Front* (Graywolf, 2006), which won an Anisfield-Wolf Award and was chosen as one of "25 Books to Remember from 2006" by the New York Public Library. Collins has also published four collections of poems, two collections of co-translations of Vietnamese poetry, and two chapbooks of poems. Founder of the Creative Writing Program at UMass Boston and Pauline Delaney Professor of Creative Writing at Oberlin College until 2007, Collins is currently editor-at-large for *FIELD* magazine and one of the editors of the Oberlin College Press. In Spring 2010, she will serve as Distinguished Visiting Writer at Cornell University.

If I Were Another: Poems
by Mahmoud Darwish
Translations from the Arabic by Fady Joudah

New York: Farrar, Straus and Giroux
Publication Date: October 2009 • 240 pages
ISBN-10: 0374174296 • ISBN-13: 978-0374174296

"Mahmoud Darwish was that rare literary phenomenon: a poet both acclaimed by critics as one of the most important poets in the Arab world and beloved by his readers. His language—lyrical and tender—helped to transform modern Arabic poetry into a living metaphor for the universal experiences of exile, loss, and identity. The poems in this collection, constructed from the cadence and imagery of the Palestinian struggle, shift between the most intimate individual experience and the burdens of history and collective memory. Brilliantly translated by Fady Joudah, *If I Were Another*—which collects the greatest epic works of Darwish's mature years—is a powerful yet elegant work by a master poet and demonstrates why Darwish was one of the most celebrated poets of his time and was hailed as the voice and conscience of an entire people."—Publisher

"Darwish was born in the village of al-Birweh in Galilee, Palestine, on March 13, 1941. His family was forced to flee to Lebanon when he was six years old, but they returned after the creation of Israel in 1948. Darwish remained in Israel until 1970, when having been jailed several times for his poetry and activism, he decided to leave Haifa for Moscow. He later lived in Cairo and by 1973 had moved to Beirut, Lebanon, where he became the cultural editor of *Palestinian Affairs*. After the Israeli invasion of Lebanon in 1982, he moved to Tunis, and then to Paris, where he settled for more than a decade until his return to Ramallah in 1996. During his years in Paris, where he published all the works of his middle period, Darwish was recognized as a world poet. In the last twelve years of his life, he lived between Amman, Jordan, and Ramallah, Palestine. Darwish wrote more than twenty books of poetry and ten of prose. His work has been translated into nearly thirty languages. Among his numerous honors are the Chevalier of the Order of Arts and Letters, the Lannan Cultural Freedom Award, the Prins Claus Award (Holland), the Golden Wreath (Macedonia), the Ibn Sina Prize, the Lotus Prize, and an honorary doctorate from the University of Chile. He died in Houston, Texas, on August 9, 2008, after complications from cardiovascular surgery." (*If I Were Another: Poems*, 2009)

Mahmoud Darwish's Lyric Epic

Fady Joudah

Palestinian-American Poet, Physician, and Translator

isdoud@yahoo.com

Abstract: This essay is a reprint of an introduction by Fady Joudah, noted Palestinian-American poet and translator of Mahmoud Darwish's poetry, to *If I Were Another* (2009), a collection of poems by Darwish translated from the Arabic by Joudah. It is republished herein courtesy of the author Fady Joudah and publisher, Farrar, Straus and Giroux, New York. According to Joudah, "*If I Were Another* is a tribute to Darwish's lyric epic, and to the essence of his "late style," the culmination of an entire life in dialogue that merges the self with its stranger, its other, in continuous renewal within the widening periphery of human grace."

When Mahmoud Darwish and I met on August 4, 2008, five days before he underwent the surgery that would end his life, he reiterated the centrality and importance *Mural* holds for this collection. In *Mural* he grasped what he feared would be his last chance to write after surviving cardiovascular death for the second time in 1999. The poem was a song of praise that affirms life and the humanity not only of the marginalized Palestinian but also of the individual on this earth, and of Mahmoud Darwish himself. *Mural* was made into a play by the Palestinian National Theatre shortly after its publication in 2000 without any prompting from Darwish (his poetry has often been set to film, music, and song). The staged poem has continued to tour the world to astounding acclaim, in Paris, Edinburgh, Tunisia, Ramallah, Haifa, and elsewhere. A consummate poet at the acme of innermost experience, simultaneously personal and universal, between the death of language and physical death, Darwish created something uniquely his: the treatise of a private speech become collective. *Mural* was the one magnum opus of which he was certain, a rare conviction for a poet who reflects on

---

Fady Joudah, a Palestinian-American poet and physician, was the 2007 winner of the Yale Series of Younger Poets Competition for his collection of poems *The Earth in the Attic*, which was published by Yale University Press in April 2008. Joudah was born in Austin, Texas, in 1971 to Palestinian refugee parents, and grew up in Libya and Saudi Arabia. He returned to the United States to study to become a doctor, first attending the University of Georgia in Athens, and then the Medical College of Georgia, before completing his medical training at the University of Texas. Joudah currently practices as an ER physician in Houston, Texas. He has also volunteered abroad with the humanitarian organization Doctors Without Borders. Joudah's poetry has been published in a variety of publications, including *Poetry* magazine, *Iowa Review, Kenyon Review, Drunken Boat, Prairie Schooner* and *Crab Orchard*. In 2006, he published *The Butterfly's Burden*, a collection of recent poems by Palestinian poet Mahmoud Darwish translated from Arabic. He was a finalist for the 2008 PEN Award for Poetry in Translation for his translation of Mahmoud Darwish's *The Butterfly's Burden* (Copper Canyon Press, 2007). The translation won the Saif Ghobash-Banipal Prize for Arabic Literary translation from the Society of Authors in the United Kingdom. **CREDIT:** Previously published as Introduction to *If I Were Another: Poems* (2009), a collection of poems by Mahmoud Darwish translated from the Arabic by Fady Joudah, this essay is republished herein courtesy of the author Fady Joudah and publisher, Farrar, Straus and Giroux, 18 West 18th Street, New York, NY 10011.

his completed works with harsh doubt equal only to his ecstatic embrace when on the threshold of new poems.

His first experience of death, in 1984, was peaceful and painless, filled with darwish. "whiteness." The second was more traumatic and was packed with intense visions. *Mural* gathered Darwish's experiences of life, art, and death, in their white serenity and violent awakening, and accelerated his "late style" into prolific, progressively experimental output in search of new possibilities in language and form, under the shadow of absence and a third and final death. "Who am I to disappoint the void / who am I" ask the final lines of *The Dice Player*, Darwish's last uncollected lyric epic, written weeks before his death on August 9, 2008. But I still remember his boyish, triumphant laugh when I said to him: "*The Dice Player* is a distilled *Mural* in entirely new diction," and his reply: "Some friends even call it the *anti-Mural*." He had overcome his own art (and death) for one last time, held it apart from himself so that it would indisputably and singularly belong to him and he to it.

If I Were Another is a tribute to Darwish's lyric epic, and to the essence of his "late style," the culmination of an entire life in dialogue that merges the self with its stranger, its other, in continuous renewal within the widening periphery of human grace. The two collections of long poems that begin this book, *I See What I Want* (1990) and *Eleven Planets* (1992), mark the completion of Darwish's middle period. In them he wove a "space for the jasmine" and (super)imposed it on the oppressive exclusivity of historical and antinomian narrative. In 1990, between the personal and the collective, "birth [was] a riddle," but in 1996 birth became "a cloud in [Darwish's] hand." And by *Mural*'s end (2000), there was "no cloud in [his] hand / no eleven planets / on [his] temple." Instead there was the vowel in his name, the letter *Waw*, "loyal to birth wherever possible." By 2005, Darwish

would return, through the medium or vision of almond blossoms, the flower of his birth in March, to revisit the memory and meaning of place, and the "I" in place, through several other selves, in *Exile*, his last collected long poem. Dialectic, lyric, and drama opened up a new space for time in his poetry, a "lateness" infused with age and survival while it does not "go gentle into that good night."

––––––––

It is necessary to read Darwish's transformation of the long poem over the most accomplished fifteen years of his life: the shift in diction from a gnomic and highly metaphoric drive to a stroll of mixed and conversational speech; the paradoxes between private and public, presence and absence; the bond between the individual and the earth, place, and nature; the illumination of the contemporary Sufi aesthetic method as the essence of poetic knowledge, on the interface of reason and the sensory, imagination and the real, the real and its vanishing where the "I" is interchangeable with (and not split from) its other; and his affair with dialogue, and theater (tragic, absurd, or otherwise) to produce a lyric epic sui generis. If Darwish's friend the great critic Edward Said had a leaning toward the novel, Darwish was undoubtedly a playwright at heart. This had been evident since his youth, whether in poems like *A Soldier Dreams of White Lilies* (written in 1967 and now a part of the Norwegian live-film-performance *Identity of the Soul* [2008], in which Darwish is featured), or *Writing to the Light of a Rifle* (1970), or in his brilliant early prose book and its title piece, *Diaries of Ordinary Sorrow* (1973).

Yet Darwish was never comfortable with looking back at his glorious past. He was an embodiment of exile, as both existential and metaphysical state, beyond the merely external, and beyond metaphor, in his interior relations with self and art. Naturally, and perhaps reflexively, Darwish expressed a fleeting reservation at my desire to include here the two older volumes *I See What I Want* and *Eleven Planets*. True, the two are linked to a larger historical reel than is *Mural* or *Exile*, since the former volumes were written during the first Palestinian Intifada, which began in 1987, a major defining event in the identity and hopes of a dispossessed people, and in response to the spectacle of the peace accords Darwish knew would follow. But more important, in these two volumes Darwish had written his *Canto General*, his *Notebook of a Return to My Native Land*, his *Omeros*, destabilizing the hegemony of myth into an inclusive, expansive humanizing lyric that soars, like a hoopoe, over a Canaanite reality and an Andalusian song, where vision is both Sufi and Sophoclean, and elegy arches over the father, the lover, and the other, as well as over a grand historical narrative and its liminal stages on this earth.

I See What I Want and *Eleven Planets* are collections concerned with vision, not image. Even their titles read as one. In the first instance of seeing, Darwish declares a singular self that creates its private lexicon of sorrow and praise and transformation into the collective: a prebiblical past, a Palestinian present, and a future where the self flies "just to fly," free from "the knot of symbols," to where compassion is "one in the nights" with "one moon for all, for both sides of the trench." In *Eleven Planets*, the self has vanished into its other, more elegiacally, and "flight" has reached 1492, the year of "the Atlantic banners of Columbus" and "the Arab's last exhalation" in Granada. The self is transfigured into "The 'Red Indian's' Penultimate Speech" and into "murdered Iraq," this most contemporary of graves, "O stone of the soul, our silence!" Throughout the two books, the oscillation between the "I" and the "we," the private and the public, is maintained in tension, in abeyance. And by the end, Darwish questions himself and his aesthetic: "The dead will not forgive those who stood, like us, perplexed / at the

edge of the well asking: Was Joseph the Sumerian our brother, our / beautiful brother, to snatch the planets of this beautiful evening from him?" It is the same beautiful Joseph (son of Jacob) who saw "eleven planets, the sun, and the moon prostrate before [him]" in the Quran, and it is the same past-future elegy of exile and expulsion, circling around to those other sadly beautiful planets "at the end of the Andalusian scene." Yet Darwish triumphs over the void with song: "O water, be a string to my guitar" and "open two windows on shadow street" because "April will come out of our sleep soon" "with the first almond blossom."

I See What I Want marks the first mature presence of the Sufi aesthetic in Darwish's oeuvre, where he will disassemble and reassemble his language, again and again, in an idea of return: wind, horse, wheat, well, dove, gazelle, echo, holm oak, anemones, chrysanthemum, or something more recognizably biographical, like "prison" in Israeli jails. In this recurrence and retreatment, in seating and unseating absence, Darwish is a prodigal between memory and history who extroverts language and the "need to say: Good Morning." Through the process, he attains illumination, not as a fixed and defined state but as the arrival at one truth constantly examined and replaced with another. "Take Care of the Stags, Father" is an elegy to his father, where the father, the "I," the grandfather, and the forefather intertwine and dissolve time, place, and identity "like anemones that adopt the land and sing her as a house for the sky." The private and psychological detail is abundant: Darwish's grandfather was his primary teacher; his father became an endlessly broken man who toiled as a hired laborer on land he owned before the creation of Israel in 1948; the horse he left behind "to keep the house company" when they fled was lost; and the "cactus" that grows on the site of each ruined Palestinian village punctures the heart.

All these details and themes and more

are a personal representation first and foremost. Yet the echo resounds a larger collective memory, Palestinian or otherwise. Darwish's fathers resembled, "by chance," the fathers of hundreds of thousand others, and his "I" also resembled another's. History is broken with an earth that "cracks its eggshell and swims between us / green beneath the clouds." And "exile" is "a land of words the pigeons carry to the pigeons," just as the self is "an exile of incursions speech delivers to speech." And the poem is ever present: "Why," "What good is the poem? / It raises the ceiling of our caves and flies from our blood to the language of doves." "Take Care of the Stags, Father" is also a praise for "chrysanthemum," an account of Darwish's profound relationship with the earth, where a different "specificity" and "dailiness" is filtered, captured, through presence and absence. Darwish was a "green" poet whose verse was shaped by flowers, trees, and animals the way people see them: "without story / the lemon blossom is born out of the lemon blossom"; as well as through the dispossessed landscape: a "return" within and without "progress."

The beautifully measured exegesis of "Truce with the Mongols by the Holm Oak Forest," and its epiphora of "holm oak," confirms the formal, thematic, and structural range in these two collections. The mesmerizing prescience in "Truce," however, is alarming. Peace is able to envision itself but, like Cassandra or Tiresias, is either punished or discredited. Thus "The Tragedy of Narcissus the Comedy of Silver" follows in monumental footsteps. Whether in its several stanzaic forms, as an early precursor of *Mural*, or in its undulation between elegy and praise, history and myth, absurdity and distress, this epic must be read with attention to its ubiquitous nuance, its "Ulysses / of paradox," its "Sufi [who] sneaks away from a woman" then asks, "Does the soul have buttocks and a waist and a shadow?" Circumstantially, as

noted, the poem is linked to the birth of the first Palestinian Intifada, "a stone scratching the sun." And if this "stone radiating our mystery" will provide fodder for many, "for both sides of the trench," who are drawn to the "political" in Darwish's poetry and life, Darwish offers a reply: "Extreme clarity is a mystery." Darwish wrote not a manifesto for return but a myth of return—where the exiles and displaced "used to know, and dream, and return, and dream, and know, and return, / and return, and dream, and dream, and return." "Bygones are bygones": "they returned / from the myths of defending citadels to what is simple in speech." "No harm befell the land" despite those who "immortalized their names with spear or mangonel ... and departed," since "none of them deprived April of its habits." "And land, like language, is inherited." And exile is "the birds that exceed the eulogy of their songs." Yet "victims don't believe their intuition" and don't "recognize their names." "Our history is their history," "their history is our history." Darwish asks if anyone managed to fashion "his narrative far from the rise of its antithesis and heroism" and answers: "No one." Still he pleads, "O hero within us ... don't rush," and "stay far from us so we can walk in you toward another ending, the beginning is damned."

Such an ending would find itself in "The Hoopoe." (And just as the two volumes *I See What I Want* and *Eleven Planets* are twins, "The Tragedy of Narcissus the Comedy of Silver" and "The Hoopoe" are twins.) Both poems are tragedies in verse. Threading the dream of return, "The Hoopoe" suspends arrival right from the start: "We haven't approached the land of our distant star yet." And despite the incessant remonstrance and the litany of pretexts by the collective voice in wandering—"Are we the skin of the earth?" "No sword remains that hasn't sheathed itself in our flesh"—the hoopoe insists on simply guiding to "a lost sky," to "vastness after vastness after vastness," and urges us to "cast the place's body" aside, because "the universe is smaller than a butterfly's wing in the courtyard of the large heart." "The Hoopoe" is based on the twelfth-century Sufi narrative epic poem *Conference of the Birds*, by Farid Addin al-Attar of Nishapur. In it a hoopoe leads all birds to the One, who turns out to be all the birds who managed to complete the journey and reach attainment. There are seven wadis on the path to attainment, the last of which is the Wadi of Vanishing, whose essence is Forgetfulness (a visible theme in Darwish's "late" poems). Darwish transforms this Sufi doctrine about God as an internal and not an external reality, a self inseparable from its other, to address exile and the (meta)physicality of identity in a work that is nothing short of a masterpiece.

Similarly, "Eleven Planets at the End of the Andalusian Scene" and "The 'Red Indian's' Penultimate Speech to the White Man" are two of Darwish's most accomplished and beloved poems. The former commemorates five hundred years of the brutal cleansing of Muslims and Jews from Spain, then leaps toward another annihilation across the Atlantic in the latter (which was excerpted and enacted in Jean-Luc Godard's movie *Notre Musique*). In both poems Darwish writes against the perpetual crimes of humans against humanity and against the earth, with the hope these crimes won't be repeated. Darwish clings to the dream of al-Andalus (of coexistence and mutual flourishing between outsiders and natives), even if he questions the reality of that dream, whether it existed "on earth … or in the poem" (still he asks us in "The 'Red Indian's' Speech" whether we would "memorize a bit of poetry to halt the slaughter"). "Granada is my body," he sings, "Granada is my country. / And I come from there." The "descent" is not the "Arab" laying claim to distant lands and a glorious past—a clichéd annotation; it is the grand illumination against the "cleansing" of the other, in revenge or otherwise, in the past or the future, embodied in the "dream" of al-

Andalus that could not save itself from the horrors of history.

While each of the eleven sections in "The Andalusian Scene" is a stand-alone poem, the entire sequence is a love poem that embraces time and place "in the departure to one essence" and touches the deep bond Darwish had with Federico García Lorca and his "bedouin moon." "The 'Red Indian's' Speech" should also be read beyond the comparative impulse or historical allegory (Darwish composed the poem after listening repeatedly to Native American chants) and as a defense against the destruction of the earth, as a celebration of the earth: "Do not kill the grass anymore, the grass has a soul in us that defends / the soul in the earth." "Our names are trees of the deity's speech, and birds that soar higher / than the rifle," so "if our murder is imperative, then do not / kill the animals that have befriended us"; "do / you know the deer will not chew the grass if our blood touches it?" "A Canaanite Rock in the Dead Sea" retreats (into) the "father" and reaffirms "I am I" in an "absence entirely trees." The lyric begins with "my poem / is a rock flying to my father as a partridge does." In Arabic, "partridge" is also the word for "skip" or "hop"—exactly the rhythm of this poem. Ablation of myth is rewritten through the Canaanite "pigeon tower" and through the sharing of the earth.

"We Will Choose Sophocles" switches to the collective in a discourse that weaves ancient and contemporary identity, a gentle living "the taste of small differences among the seasons," where "the mallow climbs the ancient shields / and its red flowers hide what the sword has done to the name." Another significance of the poem stems from the mention of two literary characters placed in opposition: Imru' el-Qyss, prince of Kinda, the great pre-Islamic (Jahili) Arab poet, who sought Caesar's help (to avenge his father's murder) and failed and died as consequence of this option; and Sophocles, who rejected and mocked political authority and power. This coincides with the looming failure of the 1993 Oslo peace accords. Darwish's invocation of the Greek dramatist's lines—"He who makes the journey / To one in power is / His salve even if when / He set out he was free"—is haunting. His rejection of the peace façade is both firm and tender, a theme he develops in a 1996 poem, "A Non-linguistic Dispute with Imru' el-Qyss": "Our blood wasn't speaking in microphones on/ that day, the day we leaned on a language that dispersed / its heart when it changed its path. No one / asked Imru' el-Qyss: What have you done / to us and to yourself? Go now on Caesar's / path, after a smoke that looks out through / time, black. Go on Caesar's path, alone, alone, alone, / and leave, right here, for us, your language!" And again later in *Mural*, with growing disinterest that highlights the mutability of recurrence or circularity in the Darwish poem: "I tired of what my language on the backs of horses / says or doesn't say about the days of Imru' el-Qyss / who was scattered between Caesar and rhyme."

The conundrum whereby the Palestinian tragedy is not permitted to "belong to the victim's question" "without interruption" clouds the reading of Darwish's poetry for many. "I am he, my self's coachman, / no horse whinnies in my language," Darwish would say in *Exile* in 2005, asserting his supreme concern with his art, independence, and individuality. Still, in "Rita's Winter," a love poem that returns us to Darwish's affair with dialogue, the private is at its most triumphant in these two collections. "Rita" is a pseudonym for Darwish's first love, a Jewish Israeli woman who became a cultural icon in the Arabic world after the renowned Lebanese musician and singer Marcel Khalife sang one of Darwish's youthful poems, "Rita and the Rifle": "There's a rifle between Rita and me / and whoever knows Rita bows / and prays / to a god in those honey eyes . . ." "O Rita / nothing could turn your eyes away from

mine / except a snooze / some honey clouds/ and this rifle." The rifle connotes the Israeli military, in which Rita enlisted (and which perhaps reappears as the handgun placed on "the poem's draft" in the final lines of "Rita's Winter"). There were at least four more Rita poems in the 1960s and 70s. In "The Sleeping Garden" in 1977, for example, Darwish wrote: "Rita sleeps . . . sleeps then wakes her dreams: / Shall we get married? / Yes. / When? / When violet grows / on the soldiers' helmet. . ." "I love you, Rita. I love you. Sleep / and I will ask you in thirteen winters: / Are you still sleeping?" Rita would sleep for fifteen additional winters before she would make her return in 1992, her final appearance in a Darwish poem.

———

As I said, *Mural's* significance stems from a great artist's engagement with death in his late years: the simultaneity of art and mortality, the objective and the subjective, on two parallel lanes of what is left of time in a body or, as Theodor Adorno termed it, "the catastrophe" of "late style" (an ironic expression for a Palestinian). *Mural* begins a period of elusive abandon in Darwish's poetry, an ease with what language may bring. He puts it another way in "I Don't Know the Stranger," a poem from 2005: "The dead are equal before death, they don't speak / and probably don't dream ... / and this stranger's funeral might have been mine / had it not been for a divine matter that postponed it / for many reasons, among them/ an error in my poem." This righting of the poem's wrong life—this potential philosophic "error" (which also shadows the eleventh-century Arab poet-philosopher al-Ma'arri) upon which Darwish embarked—was a chronic concern for him. In *Mural*, certain elements of his youthful aesthetic, namely dialogue and more casual diction, return and are now redeemed by age. Pithy narrative stitches the lyric epic into drama on the stage. Monologue belongs to several voices. Darwish's dramatic theater (of "The Tragedy of Narcissus" or "The Hoopoe") incorporates several styles of dialogue and quotidian settings. For example, the terse, concise line-by-line chat between Darwish and his prison guard toward the poem's end is a continuation of the conversational tone that resurfaced in short lyrics in *Why Did You Leave the Horse Alone?* (1996), was mastered in *Don't Apologize for What You've Done* (2003), and became fully available in the lyric epic in *Exile* (2005).

Mural rotates setting and scene in three major movements between a hospital room, Death, and the poet's visions and conversations. The poem opens with the nurse and the poet's "horizontal" name, Darwish's awareness of his death, his ensuing search for meaning and existence. He becomes "the dialogue of dreamers," a bird, a vineyard, and a poet whose language is "a metaphor for metaphor." But the nurse swiftly returns and interrupts him in an important moment that heralds the full realization of the name in the final pages of *Mural* (when the "horizontal name" becomes vertical abecedary). For now, however, a woman nurse says: "This is your name, remember it well! / And don't disagree with it over a letter / or concern yourself with tribal banners, / be a friend to your horizontal name, / try it out on the dead and the living, teach it / accurate pronunciation in the company of strangers," "a stranger is another stranger's brother. / We will seize the feminine with a vowel promised to the flutes." Then Darwish is reunited with his first love, his first goddess and first legends, his stranger self, his "other" and "alternate."

Early in the poem Darwish (who was shy, generous, and modest) is quite aware of the unfolding play that has become his life, between perception and illusion, the private and the public, poem and being: "Am I he? / Do I perform my role well in the final act?" "or did the victim change / his affidavit to live the postmodern moment, / since the author strayed from the script / and the actors and spectators have gone?" Characters (including "echo" and "Death") enter and exit the lyrical fantasy of the poet. He is "one who talks to himself" and one who "sang to weigh the spilled vastness / in the ache of a dove." And he arrives at an essential truth of his art: "my poem's land is green and high," a celebration of being alive, and of the earth, because "there is no nation smaller than its poem," and "the earth is the festival of losers" to whom Darwish belongs (perhaps as the absented poet of Troy). And he returns to his poem's features: "the narcissus contemplating the water of its image," "the clarity of shadows in synonyms," "the speech of prophets on the surface of night," "the donkey of wisdom ... mocking the poem's reality and myth," "the congestion of symbol with its opposites," "the other 'I' / writing its diaries in the notebooks of lyricists ... at the gates of exile," and "echo as it scrapes the sea salt / of [his] language off the walls." The nurse reenters, and the poet catalogs visions and dreams induced by sedatives: memories of his father's death, his mother's bread, his exile from his language and place, and his kinship to dead poets and philosophers. He realizes he is still alive, that his "hour hasn't arrived," and summons his favorite goddess, Anat, to sing since "life might come suddenly, / to those disinclined to meaning, from the wing of a butterfly / caught in a rhyme."

"And I want to live," he declares to begin the second and perhaps best-known movement of *Mural*. This vivid and occasionally humorous dialogue with Death is timeless writing. Darwish is neither waiting for Godot nor bargaining with Faustus. He leaves us his will (which he knows will not be followed when he dies), perhaps to authenticate the separateness of his private self from what the larger collective perceives it to be (though in death, the gap becomes narrow): "Death! wait for me, until I finish / the funeral arrangements in this fragile spring, / when I was born, when I would prevent the sermonizers / from repeating what they said about the sad country / and the resistance of olives and figs in the face / of time and its army. I will tell them: Pour me / in the *Nu n*, where my soul gulps / Surat al-Rahman in the Quran," and "Don't put violets on my grave: violets are / for the depressed, to remind the dead of love's / premature death. Put seven green ears / of wheat on the coffin instead, and some / anemones, if either can be found. Otherwise, leave the roses / of the church to the church and the weddings. / Death, wait, until I pack my suitcase: / my toothbrush, my soap, / my electric razor, cologne, and clothes. / Is the climate temperate there? / Do conditions change in the eternal whiteness / or do they remain the same in autumn / as in winter? Is one book enough / to entertain me in timelessness, or will I need / a library? And what's the spoken language there: / colloquial for all, or classical Arabic?"

With irony and resolve, Darwish embraces and humanizes the self and others, where he is simultaneously a lyrical letter in the Quran and "at ease with the Old Testament's narrative" as the beautiful Joseph, whose vision is of abundance and fertility in "seven green ears / of wheat." Even Arabic is an "I" indivisible from its "other," an "exterior" within an "interior." And as Darwish goes on in this wonderful dialogue with Death, paradox and parody ("Death, wait, have a seat," "perhaps / the star wars have tired you today?") grow into exultation ("all the arts have defeated you") and provocation ("you are the only exile, poor you," "How do you walk like this without guards or a singing choir, / like a coward thief"). But this frivolity does not last long, and the poet comes clean with Death because the two of them "on god's road / are two Sufis who are governed by vision / but don't see." Still, Darwish insists, despite Death's indifference, on meeting by the sea gate, where the poem will eventually close, in Akko, the port of his childhood, seven kilo-

meters from his razed village, al-Birweh, in Galilee. And as with the hospital scene and the name, "this sea" will eventually become present to announce the poem's end.

The third movement begins as the nurse reappears and "the death of language" has passed. In one of the poem's more memorable stanzas, in a recurring scene between patient and nurse, she says to him: "You used to hallucinate / often and scream at me: / I don't want to return to anyone, / I don't want to return to any country / after this long absence … / I only want to return / to my language in the distances of cooing." In this extreme moment of personality disconcerted with geographical "return," in the artist's tremendous and volatile gripping of his medium, "the distances of cooing," their quietude and serene imagination, paradoxically affirm "return" to a region beyond the political or historical, therefore more lasting, more durable. The poem remains "green and high," and the poet writes it down "patiently, to the meter / of seagulls in the book of water," and "to the scattering / of wheat ears in the book of the field." Again he praises: "I am the grain / of wheat that has died to become green again. / And in my death there is a kind of life …" And as is Darwish's custom of uniting art with life, he tells us of what he has fathered: "I preferred the free marriage between words … / the feminine will find the suitable masculine / in poetry's leaning toward prose …" Between "the sentimental" and "thousands of romantic years" the poet carves "a tattoo in identity" where "The personal is not personal. / The universal not universal …"

Darwish returns to myth, the mirror image of the poem's first movement, a circular aesthetic. Anat, the Sumerian and Canaanite goddess, reappears, scriptures persist, but new characters and subjects also appear: Gilgamesh, Enkidu, Osiris, King Solomon, and the Book of Ecclesiastes. He meets his boy self, his girl love, his prison guard, and his childhood horse. With each encounter Darwish rewrites anew what he had written in the past (as in the story of his imprisonment) or what he would rewrite in the future (as in the horse that guided his family back to an unconscious boy Darwish who fell off it one wild night when he took it out for a ride). Perhaps "the horse" exemplifies the excessive reading that frequently goes into Darwish's "symbols," whereas in fact these "symbols" are often private memories. Perhaps it is the same horse who saved Darwish's life that the poet addresses toward the end of *Mural*: "Persist, my horse, we no longer differ in the wind … / you're my youth and I'm your imagination. Straighten / like an *Aleph*," "You're my pretext, and I'm your metaphor / away from riders who are tamed like destinies." Perhaps it is an appeal to that elemental bond that granted him life once that it might grant it again, in a delightful dance between the pastoral and the postmodern: "Don't die before me, horse, or after me, or with me / on the final slope. And look inside the ambulances, / stare at the dead … I might still be living."

The plethora of actors and dialogue accelerate, and gather, suspense in a radiance that lends itself to the imagination on the stage. And in preparation for the finale, Darwish announces that "as Christ walked on the lake, / I walked in my vision. But I came down / from the cross because I have a fear of heights and don't / promise resurrection. I only changed / my cadence to hear my heart clearly." This declaration of his fragility goes on to speak the most delicate assertion of his poetry: "The epicists have falcons, and I have /*The Collar of the Dove*," the wings of love that would return him to Akko's port, as he had mentioned in an earlier poem, "Ivory Combs," where his "mother had lost her handkerchiefs"; or maybe it is as he retells it in *Mural*: "I might /add the description of Akko to the story / the oldest beautiful city / the loveliest old city / a stone box / where the dead and the living move / in its clay as if in a captive

beehive." Darwish begins the final ascension of *Mural* and recounts what is his, starting with Akko's sea, his semen, and down to the two meters of this earth that would house his 175-centimeter horizontal body, and his return to his horizontal name, now loosened into vertical lines whose alliterative luminosity will remain the privacy of his language, the language of the *Dhad*, impossible to translate otherwise. And the simply complex notion of his existence, and of anyone's being, becomes an eternal calling: "I am not mine / I am not mine / I am not mine."

———

Six years and three books after *Mural*, in 2005, Darwish was still writing, still searching for the self within its others, through new lyric form. *Exile* is a play in verse that "neither linger[s] … nor hurr[ies]" in a mature prosody like "life's simple prose," even if intransigently lyrical and giddy in parts. *Exile* has its "bridge" and could simply be "the cunning of eloquence" or "the backdrop of the epic scene." And "return" is "a comedy by one of our frivolous goddesses." If dialogue or dialectic and its supporting cast were spontaneous and major expressions in the totality of Darwish's language in *Mural*, they became a more purposeful aesthetic of the theater of the lyric epic in *Exile*: four quartets, each with a setting and at least two characters, palpable or spectral, named or unnamed (of which the "I" is constant among them); choral modes or interludes are regularly introduced (especially in the first three movements); memory and vision stand in for scenes within each act; the entire sequence is a dialogue that alternates between the absurd and the expository. *Exile* walks in strata or polyphony: of love and pleasure ("If the canary doesn't sing / to you, my friend"); of place ("What is place?" "The senses' discovery of a foothold / for intuition"); of time (where one and his ghost "fly, as a Sufi does, in the words … to anywhere"); and of art (where "aesthetic is only the presence / of the real in form," "a freedom" that bids "farewell to the poem / of pain").

The first quartet finds the poet strolling on a Tuesday when "the weather is clear" "as if [he] were another." After remembrance and forgetting, and wonderful discursiveness, he meets his lover. ("My lexicon is Sufi. My desires are sensory / and I am not who I am / unless the two meet: / I and the feminine I," he would write in *The Dice Player* in 2008.) Unlike Rita, the "feminine" in "Tuesday and the Weather Is Clear" is not named, yet the personal detail is equally intimate, if not more so. And as the two part, the poet continues to walk until he finds himself in the throes of his private language and conducts a brilliant appeal to it, almost a prayer: "O my language, / help me to adapt and embrace the universe"; "My language, will I become what you'll become, or are you / what becomes of me? Teach me the wedding parade / that merges the alphabet with my body parts. / Teach me to become a master not an echo"; "For who, if I utter what isn't poetry, / will understand me? Who will speak to me of a hidden / longing for a lost time if I utter what isn't poetry? / And who will know the stranger's land?..."

In the second sequence, the self moves into its masculine other "on the bridge," where fog competes with vision at dawn. A dialectic, where "a thing cannot be known by its opposite," dominates "Dense Fog over the Bridge," which pushes the limits of obsession and rumination until it delivers perhaps the last intense lyric spell in Darwish's poetry, a dream approaching "fever" in sixteen successive quatrains that speak of jasmine and "every -ology" until the "I" reaches "the land of story." "Dense Fog" certainly invokes the Jericho Bridge (formerly the Allenby Bridge, after the British general who conquered Jerusalem in 1917). The bridge has become iconic for Palestinians and continues to serve as an oppressive checkpoint for those crossing between Jordan and the West Bank. It was on this bridge, for example, that Darwish was recently interrogated and asked, as the famous poet, to recite some of his poems, to which he replied: "A prisoner does not sing to his prison warden."

Darwish managed to transform this subjugation into a more profound dialogue in his poetry, where the physicality of the bridge, and of those on it, is and is not itself. (Like "river," the manifestation of "bridge" in Darwish's late poetry is worthy of independent study. See, for example, "We Walk on the Bridge," or the occurrence of "river" in poems like "A Cloud from Sodom" or "A Mask ... for Majnoon Laila.") Recurrence simply seeks "the thing itself," or, as he said in "The Southerner's House" in 2003, "the transparency of the thing." And the journey home becomes more beautiful than home: "On the bridge," the mystery that was "extreme clarity" in "The Tragedy of Narcissus" becomes "neither mysterious nor clear," "like a dawn that yawns a lot." And Jericho (which was one of the first cities handed over to "Palestinian control" under the "peace agreement") is simply exposed: "Don't promise me anything / don't give me / a rose from Jericho." Darwish was looking "not for a burial place" but "a place to live in, to curse" if he wished it so. Short of that, he would continue to rotate on "the bridge," between entry and exit, interior and exterior, "like a sunflower," while absence is still "wearing trees." And he would be content with the "work [he has left] to do in myth."

And walking farther, toward this new task in myth, Darwish stumbles onto his ghost, his shadow, the archetypal exile, the wandering human, personified in the pre-Islamic Arab poet Tarafah Ibn al-Abd (who is also mentioned in *Mural*, and paired with "existentialists"). The title of the poem, "Like a Hand Tattoo in the Jahili Poet's Ode," draws from the opening line of Tarafah's famous ode, which describes the ruins of the beloved's dwelling that "sway like the remnants of a tattoo on the back of a hand." The poem is suspended between two shadows of the same self, one that urges the other to "drop metaphor, and take a stroll on the woolly earth," while the other is deceived by "a cloud [that] knits its identity around [him]." This paradox is held in balance between "two epochs": the first "imagination's return to the real," the relics of "an ancestral notion," and the second "a butterfly trace in the light." (Thus "Hand Tattoo" is significant as an *ars poetica* that combines two major aesthetics of the history of Arab poetics in one poem.)

Darwish's easing of the lyric intensity takes hold in "Hand Tattoo" (and prepares the reader for "Counterpoint," the final quartet). The poem addresses the marginalized account of the Palestinian narrative in more personal and informal speech. "And as for anthem, the anthem of happy finale / has no poet." A third voice is eventually introduced. It grounds dialogue between the two, like "a bulldozer / driver who changed the spontaneity of this place / and cut the braids of your olive trees to match / the soldiers' hair." Governed by silence and absence, pointed dialogue follows. The struggle to break free from the shackles of identity in "Hand Tattoo" remains as it was in "The Hoopoe": "Place is the passion." And flight "in the words ... to anywhere" also persists. Still the "I and I" seek to "make amends" with their relics, since "in the presence of death we grasp only the accuracy of our names," a quotidian existentiality that is sieved through the mystery of identity. However, in time, "I and I" "found not one stone / that carries a victim's name," "a lewd absurdity."

Darwish does not resolve the poem and takes myth into the satiric final lines, which expose the eroticization of a place and its people, no matter how language subverts the plot of power. If Darwish had previously attempted to upend myth and history, through the affirmation of the ancient (Canaanite) self, and through

fraternity with a larger human narrative, he now comes full circle to the "lewd absurdity" that turns a victim into a new fascination of a "foreign tourist who loves [the native's] myths" and would love "to marry one of [his goddess's] widowed daughters." It's a startling ending of a very serious poem, a determined "frivolous" conclusion, in fact, and it returns us to the poem's beginning, when the poet wished his name had "fewer letters, / easier letters on the foreign woman's ears," a spoof and an almost elegiac reverberation of the nurse's instruction to Darwish regarding his name at the beginning of *Mural*.

This amusement and irreconcilability, this "late style," is a highly developed form of aesthetic resistance ("Every beautiful poem is an act of resistance," Darwish later wrote). It is fitting, therefore, that in the final movement of *Exile*, Edward Said appears, side by side with Darwish, where, on the one hand, "the intellectual reins in the novelist's rendition," and on the other, "the philosopher dissects the singer's rose." The two protagonists converge and part over exile as "two in one / like a sparrow's wings," in diction that seems like talk over coffee or dinner. Identity is exposed as "self-defense" that should not be "an inheritance / of a past" but is what its "owner creates": "I am the plural. Within my interior / my renewing exterior resides." And Darwish's final lines, his "farewell to the poem / of pain," embrace "the impossible" and "the suitable," "words / that immortalize their readers," one of the legacies he leaves behind and entrusts to us.

———

For the longest time I have been drawn to a passage on "intention" in Theodor Adorno's *Minima Moralia*. He talks about film, image, and reproduction, but the passage also brings to mind the "use" or "function" of poetry: "True intentions would only be possible by renouncing intention," Adorno says, and this "stems from the [ambiguous] concept of significance." Significance hits the mark when "the objective figure, the realized expression, turns outward from itself and speaks"; equally, significance goes astray when "the figure is corrupted by counting in the interlocutor." This "danger" must be undertaken in a work of art: "Significant form, however esoteric, makes concessions to consumption; lack of significance is dilettantism by its immanent criteria. Quality is decided by the depth at which the work incorporates the alternatives within itself, and so masters them."

This seems to me a profound account of Darwish's work. Intention in his poetry gives way to language, in lyric form, without ever losing significance, despite the hazardous paradox of public appropriation of the work, which Darwish always guarded against by engaging several other selves; a spherical form, or an "orbit I never lose," as he said in "Hand Tattoo." "There is no love that is not an echo," Adorno says in another entry, and so it is for Darwish. Echo is return. Echo is reciprocity, and also the distance necessary for the "I" to reach its "other," for the "other" to recognize its "I." At a book signing for *Like Almond Blossoms or Farther* in Ramallah, 2005, Darwish wrote: "The Palestinian is not a profession or a slogan. He, in the first place, is a human being who loves life and is taken by almond blossoms and feels a shiver after the first autumn rain," "and this means the long occupation has failed to erase our human nature, and has not succeeded in submitting our language and emotions to the drought desired for them at the checkpoint." "Words are not land or exile" but the "density of a stanza that isn't written with letters" and "the yearning to describe the whiteness of almond blossoms."

Darwish would not neglect "the poem's end," he would leave "the door open/ for the Andalus of lyricists, and [choose] to stand / on the almond and pomegranate fence, shaking / the spiderwebs off [his]

grandfather's aba / while a foreign army was marching / the same old roads, measuring time/with the same old war machine." He clearly merges East and West (where "the East is not completely East/and the West is not completely West"), and the repetitive processing and expansion of lexicon and memory stand for a philosophy. The list of great writers who inform his poetry (or coincide with it, and he with theirs) is not merely a reflection of influence but an assertion of the shared well of human knowledge and spirit. "A poet is made up of a thousand poets," he used to say. He became deeply enmeshed in the complex, rich history of Arabic literary thought as he wrote a language for his time. His treatment of dialectic, metaphysics, mysticism, recurrence, form, duality, among other things, and deserves more advanced study than I can offer, but it also demands a daring, unapologetic openness to life, humanity, and the world: "If I were another I would have belonged to the road", "become two / on this road: I ... and another"; "If I were another I would leave this white paper and converse with a Japanese novel whose author climbs to the mountaintop to see what predator and marauder birds have done with his ancestors. Perhaps he is still writing, and his dead are still dying. But I lack the experience, and the metaphysical harshness"; "if I were another / I might still be myself the second time around."

SOURCES

Adonis, *Sufism and Surrealism* (Saqi Books, 2005).
Theodor Adorno, *Minima Moralia* (Verso, 1974).
Sinan Anton, "Mahmoud Darwish's Allegorical Critique of Oslo," *Journal of Palestine Studies*, 2002.
Mahmoud Darwish, *The Butterfly's Burden* (Copper Canyon Press, 2007).
Reginald Gibbons, "Sophokles the Poet," *American Poetry Review*, 2008.
Georg Lukács, *The Historical Novel* (Merlin Press, 1989).
Edward W. Said, *On Late Style: Music and the Literature Against the Grain* (Vintage, 2008).

The "Red Indian's" Penultimate Speech to the White Man

Mahmoud Darwish

Translation by Fady Joudah

Did I say, The Dead?
There is no Death here,
there is only a change of worlds.
—Duwamish Chief Seattle

1.

Then, we are who we are in the Mississippi. We have what is left to us of yesterday
     But the sky's color has changed, and the sea to the east
has changed, master of white ones! horse master, so what do you want
from those who are going to the trees of the night?
     Our souls are high, our pastures sacred, and the stars
are illuminated speech ... if you stare into them you would read our story entire:
we were born here between water and fire ... and will become reborn
in the clouds at the edge of the lapis coast after resurrection ... soon.
So do not kill the grass anymore, the grass has a soul in us that defends
the soul in the earth
     Horse master! train your horse to apologize
     to nature's soul for what you have done to our trees:
     Ah! my tree my sister
     they have tortured you as they have tortured me
     do not ask forgiveness
     for the logger of your mother and mine ...

2.

... The white master will not understand the ancient words
here, in spirits emancipated between trees and sky ...
because Columbus the free has the right to find India in any sea,
and the right to name our ghosts as pepper or Indian,
and he is able to break the compass of the sea then mend it
along with the errors of the northerly wind. But he doesn't believe

CREDIT: Darwish, Mahmoud. 2009. "The 'Red Indian's' Penultimate Speech to the White Man." Pp. 69-77 in *If I Were Another* by Mahmoud Darwish. Translation from the Arabic by Fady Joudah. New York: Farrar, Straus and Goroux. Gratefully reprinted by permission from the publisher of the poem.

humans are equal like air and water outside the map's kingdom!
And that they are born as people are born in Barcelona, though they worship
nature's god in everything … and do not worship gold …
Columbus the free searches for a language he did not find here,
and for gold in our kind ancestors' skulls, he did
as he pleased with the dead and the living in us. Why then
does he still see this annihilation from his grave to its end?
Nothing remains of us but an ornament of ruin, and light feathers
on the garments of the lakes. You have burst seventy million hearts … enough,
enough for you to return from our death as monarch of the new time …
isn't it time we met, stranger, as two strangers of one time
and one land, the way strangers meet by a chasm?
We have what is ours … and we have what is yours of sky.
You have what is yours … and what is ours of air and water.
We have what we have of pebbles … and you have what you have of iron.
Come, let's split the light in the force of shadow, take what you want
of the night, and leave two stars for us to bury our dead in their orbit,
take what you want of the sea, and leave two waves for us to fish in,
take the gold of the earth and the sun, and leave the land of our names
and go back, stranger, to your kin … and look for India

3.

… Our names are trees of the deity's speech, and birds that soar higher
than the rifle. Do not sever the trees of the name, you comers
from the sea in war, and do not exhale your horses aflame in the plains,
you have your god and we have ours. You have your faith and we have ours.
So do not bury god in books that promised you a land in our land
as you claim, and do not make your god a chamberlain in the royal court!
Take the roses of our dreams to see what we see of joy!
And sleep in the shadow of our willows to fly like pigeons
as our kind ancestors flew and returned in peace.
You will lack, white ones, the memory of departure from the Mediterranean
you will lack eternity's solitude in a forest that doesn't look upon the chasm
you will lack the wisdom of fractures, the setback of war
you will lack a rock that doesn't obey the rapid flow of time's river
you will lack an hour of meditation in anything that might ripen in you
a necessary sky for the soil, you will lack an hour of hesitation between one path
and another, you will lack Euripides one day, the Canaanite and the Babylonian
poems and Solomon's songs of Shulamit, and you will lack the lily of longing
you will lack, white ones, a memory that tames the horses of madness
and a heart that scratches the rock to burnish itself on the violins' calling …
you will lack the confusion of the gun: if our murder is imperative, then do not
kill the animals that have befriended us, and do not kill our yesterday
you will lack a truce with our ghosts in the barren winter nights
and you will lack a dim sun, a gibbous moon, for the crime to appear
less festive on the movie screen, so take your time
to kill god …

4.

… We know what this ambiguous rhetoric conceals for us.
A sky descending on our salt pacifies the soul. A willow
walking afoot the wind, a beast founding a kingdom in
the vacuoles of wounded space … and a sea salting our wooden doors.
The earth wasn't any heavier before creation, but we knew something
like this existed before time … the wind will narrate to us
our beginning and end. Yet today we hemorrhage our present
and bury our days in the ashes of legend. Athena is not ours,
we know your days from the smoke of the place. Athena is not yours,
we know what the master-metal prepared for our sake
and for the sake of gods that did not defend the salt in our bread.
And we know that fact is stronger than truth, that time
has changed when the weapons changed. So who will raise our voices
to a brittle rain in the clouds? Who will wash the light after us
and who will dwell in our temple after us? Who will preserve our rituals
from the metallic roar? "We promise you civilization," the stranger said,
and said: I am the master of time, I have come to inherit your earth,
pass before me, to count you corpse by corpse over the face of the lake.
"I promise you civilization," he said, to revive the gospels, he said, so pass
for god to remain mine alone, dead Indians are better
to the lord in his heights than living Indians, the lord is white
and white is this day: you have a world and we have a world …
The stranger says strange words, and digs a well in the earth
to bury the sky in it. The stranger says strange words
and hunts our children and the butterflies.
What have you promised our garden, stranger?
Some tin roses prettier than our roses? Do what you please, but do
you know the deer will not chew the grass if our blood touches it?
Do you know the buffalo and the plants are our brothers?
Do not dig the earth any deeper! Do not wound the turtle whose back
the earth, our grandmother the earth, sleeps upon, our trees are her hair,
and our adornment her flower. "There is no death in this earth," do not change
her fragile creation! Do not break the mirrors of her gardens,
or startle her, do not hurt the earth. Our rivers are her waist
and we are her grandchildren, we and you, so do not kill her …
We will be gone, in a little while, so take our blood and leave her
as she is,
　　　　as god's most beautiful writing on the water,
　　　　　　　　　　　　　　leave her for him … and for us.
We will hear our ancestors' voices in the wind, and listen
to their pulse in our tree buds. This earth is our grandmother,
all of it is sacred, stone by stone, this land is a hut
for gods that dwell within us, star by star, and illuminate for us
the prayer nights … We walked barefoot to touch the soul of pebbles,
and we marched naked for the soul, the soul of the air, to wear us as women
who give back nature's gifts—our history is her history. Time had enough

time for us to be born in her, and return from and to her: we patiently give back
to the earth her souls. And we preserve the memories of our loved ones in jars
of oil and salt, we used to hang their names on the birds of the creeks.
We were the first, there was no ceiling between the sky and the blue of our doors,
there were no horses chewing the grass of our deer in the fields, no strangers
passing through the nights of our wives, so leave a flute behind for the wind to cry
over the wounded people of this place … and over you tomorrow,
to cry … over you … tomorrow!

5.

And as we bid our fires farewell, we don't return the greeting …
Don't write the decrees of the new god, the iron god, upon us, and don't ask
the dead for a peace treaty, none of them remain
to promise you peace with the self and others, we had
longevity here, before England's rifles, before French wine
and influenza, we used to live as we should live, companions of the gazelle.
We memorized our oral history, we used to promise you innocence and daisies,
you have your god and we have ours, you have your past and we have ours,
and time is a river, when we stare into the river time wells up within us …
Will you not memorize a bit of poetry to halt the slaughter?
Were you not born of women? Did you not suckle as we did
the milk of longing for mothers? Did you not wear wings as we did
to join the swallows? We used to announce spring to you
so don't draw your weapons! We can exchange some gifts and some songs.
My nation was here. My nation died here. Here the chestnut trees
hide my nation's souls. My nation will return as air and light and water,
so take my mother's land by sword, I won't sign my name
to the peace treaty between the murdered and his killer, I won't sign my name
to the purchase of a single hand's breadth of thorn around the cornfields,
I know that I bid the last sun farewell, and that I wrap myself with my name
to fall into the river, I know I will come back to my mother's heart for you
to enter, master of white ones, your age … Raise, then, above
my corpse the freedom statutes that do not return the greeting, and chisel
the iron cross on my rocky shadow, I will ascend in a little while the summits
of song, the song of group suicides that parade their history to the far,
and I will release the voices of our birds into them: right here
the strangers conquered salt, the sea merged with clouds, and the strangers
conquered the wheat chaff in us, laid out lines for lightning and electricity,
here the eagle died depressed in suicide, here the strangers conquered
us. And nothing remains for us in the new time.
Here our bodies evaporate, cloud by cloud, into space.
Here our souls glitter, star by star, in the space of song!

6.

A long time will pass for our present to become a past like us.
But first, we will march to our doom, we will defend the trees we wear
and defend the bell of the night, and a moon we desire over our huts.

We will defend the imprudence of our gazelles, the clay of our pots
and our feathers in the wings of the final songs. In a little while
you will erect your world upon our world: from our cemeteries
you will open the road to the satellite moon. This is the age of industry. This
is the age of minerals, and out of coal the champagne of the strong will dawn …
There are dead and settlements, dead and bulldozers, dead
and hospitals, dead and radar screens that capture the dead
who die more than once in life, screens that capture the dead
who live after death, and the dead who breed the beast of civilization as death,
and the dead who die to carry the earth after the relics …
Where, master of white ones, do you take my people … and your people?
To what abyss does this robot loaded with planes and plane carriers
take the earth, to what spacious abyss do you ascend?
You have what you desire: the new Rome, the Sparta of technology
          and the ideology
                    of madness,
but as for us, we will escape from an age we haven't yet prepared our anxieties for.
We will move to the land of birds as a flock of previous humans
and look upon our land through its pebbles, through holes in the clouds,
look upon our land through the speech of stars
and through the air of the lakes, through the fragile corn fuzz
and the tomb's flower, through poplar leaves, through everything
that besieges you, white ones, we will look, as dying dead, as dead
who live, dead who return, who disclose the secrets,
so grant the earth respite until it tells the truth, all the truth,
about you
and us …

7.

There are dead who sleep in rooms you will build
there are dead who visit their past in places you demolish
there are dead who pass over bridges you will construct
there are dead who illuminate the night of butterflies, dead
who come by dawn to drink their tea with you, as peaceful
as your rifles left them, so leave, you guests of the place,
some vacant seats for your hosts … they will read you
the terms of peace … with the dead!

Tuesday and the Weather is Clear

Mahmoud Darwish

Translation by Fady Joudah

Tuesday, clear weather, I walk on a side road
covered by a ceiling of chestnut trees, I walk lightly
as if I have evaporated from my body, as if I have
a meeting with one of the poems. Distracted,
I look at my watch and flip through the pages
of faraway clouds in which the sky inscribes
higher notions. I turn matters of my heart over
to walnut trees: vacancies, without electricity,
like a small hut on a seashore. Faster, slower, faster
I walk. I stare at the billboards on either side
but don't memorize the words. I hum
a slow melody as the unemployed do:
      "The river runs like a colt to his fate / the sea, and the birds
      snatch seeds from the shoulder of the river."
I obsess and whisper to myself: Live
your tomorrow now. No matter how long you live you won't
reach tomorrow … tomorrow has no land … and dream
slowly … no matter how often you dream you'll realize
the butterfly didn't burn to illuminate you.

Light-footed I walk and look around me
hoping to see a simile between the adjectives of my self
and the willows of this space. But I discern
nothing that points to me.

      If the canary doesn't sing
      to you, my friend … know that
      you are the warden of your prison,

CREDIT: Darwish, Mahmoud. 2009. "Tuesday and the Weather is Clear." Pp. 149-159 in *If I Were Another* by Mahmoud Darwish. Translation from the Arabic by Fady Joudah. New York: Farrar, Straus and Goroux. Gratefully reprinted by permission from the publisher of the poem.

if the canary doesn't sing to you.
There is no land as narrow as a pot for roses
like your land … and no land as wide
as a book like your land … and your vision
is your exile in a world where shadow
has no identity or gravity.

You walk as if you were another.

If I could speak to anyone
on the road I would say: My privacy is what
doesn't lead to me, and it isn't a dream
of death. If I could speak to a woman
on the road I would say: My privacy doesn't
draw attention: some calcified arteries
in the feet, that's all, so walk
gently with me as a cloud walks:
"Neither linger … nor hurry …"

If I could speak to the ghost of death
behind the dahlia fence, I would say: We were born
together as twins, my brother, my murderer,
my road engineer on this earth … this earth
is my mother and yours, so drop your weapon.

And if I could speak to love, after lunch,
I would say: We were the panting of two hands
over the lint of words, when we were young,
we were the fainting of words on two knees.
And you were with few features, many

movements, and clearer: your face an angel's
face waking from sleep, your body
ram-strong like a fever. And you used to be called
what you were, "Love," and we
would swoon with night.

I walk lightly and grow older by ten minutes,
by twenty, sixty, I walk and life diminishes
in me gently as a slight cough does.
I think: What if I lingered, what
if I stopped? Would I stop time?
Would I bewilder death? I mock the notion
and ask myself: Where do you walk to
composed like an ostrich? I walk
as if life is about to amend its shortcomings.
And I don't look behind, for I can't return

to anything, and I can't masquerade as another.
If I could speak to the Lord I would say:
God! Why have you forsaken me?
I am only your shadow's shadow on earth,
how could you let me fall into the trap of questions:
why the mosquito, O God?

I walk without a rendezvous, vacant
of my tomorrow's promises. I remember that I forgot,
and I forget as I remember:

I forget a raven on an olive branch
and remember an oil stain on my pants.

I forget the gazelle's call to his mate
and remember the ant line on the sand.

I forget my longing for a star that has fallen from my hand
and remember the fur of a fox.

I forget the ancient road to our house
and remember a passion like mandarin.

I forget the things I've said
and remember what I haven't said yet.

I forget my grandfather's stories and a sword on a wall
and remember my fear of sleep.

I forget a young woman's grape-filled lips
and remember the scent of lettuce on fingers.

I forget the houses that inscribed my narrative
and remember my identity card number.

I forget grand events and a destructive shake of earth
and remember my father's tobacco in the closet.

I forget the roads of departure to a deficient void
and remember the light of planets in the bedouin atlas.

I forget the whizzing of bullets in a village that is now deserted
and remember the cricket sound in the shrub.

I forget as I remember, or I remember that I forgot.

But I remember today,
Tuesday

and the weather is clear.

And I walk on a street that doesn't lead
to a goal. Maybe my steps would guide me
to an empty bench in the garden, or
to an idea about the loss of truth between the aesthetic
and the real. I sit alone as if I had a meeting with one
of imagination's women. I imagine that I waited for long,
got bored with waiting, then exploded when she arrived:
Why were you late?! She lies and says:
It was too crowded on the bridge, settle down…
So I settle down as she fondles my hair, and I feel
the garden is our room and the shadows our curtains:

> If the canary doesn't sing
> to you, my friend … know that
> you have overslept
> if the canary doesn't sing to you.

What are you saying? she asks.
I say: The canary didn't sing to me, but do you
recall who I am, stranger? Do I resemble the ancient
pastoral poet who the stars crowned as king of the night …
the one who renounced his throne when the stars
sent him as a shepherd for clouds?

She says: If today resembles yesterday,
you seem to be you …

> There, on the opposite wooden bench,
> waiting crumbles a young woman
> who cries
> and drinks a glass of juice …
> She brightens the crystal of my small heart
> and carries for me the emotions of this day.

I ask her: How did you get here?
She says: By chance. I was walking
on a street that doesn't lead to a goal.
I say: I walk as if I have a rendezvous …
maybe my steps would guide me to an empty bench
in the garden, or to an idea about the loss of truth
between the imaginary and the real.
She asks: So you, too, recall who I am, stranger?
Do I resemble yesterday's woman, that young one
with a braid and short songs about our love

after a good long sleep?
I say: You seem to be you ...

       Over there a boy enters
       through the garden gate
       carrying twenty-five irises
       to the woman who has waited for him.
       He carries, instead of me, the youth of this day:
       This heart, my heart, is small
       and the love, my love, is large.
       It travels in the wind, descends,
       loosens a pomegranate then falls
       in the wandering of two almond
       eyes, then ascends in the dawn
       of two dimples and forgets
       the way back to house and name.
       This heart, my heart, is small
       and the love is large ...

Was he the one I was
or was I the one I wasn't?

She asks: Why do the clouds scratch the treetops?
I say: For one leg to cling to another beneath the drizzle.

—Why does a frightened cat stare at me?
—For you to put an end to the storm.

—Why does the stranger long for his yesterday?
—For poetry to depend on itself.

—Why does the sky become ashen at twilight?
—Because you didn't water the flowers in the pot.

—Why do you exaggerate your satire?
—For song to eat a bit of bread every now and then.

—Why do we love then walk on empty roads?
—To conquer the plenitude of death with less death and escape the abyss.

—Why did I dream I saw a sparrow in my hand?
—Because you're in need of someone.

—Why do you remind me of a tomorrow I do not see you in?
—You're one of eternity's features.

—You will walk alone to the tunnel of night when I'm gone.

—I will walk alone to the tunnel of night when you're gone.

… and I walk,
heavy as if I have an appointment with one of the defeats.
I walk, and a poet in me readies himself for his eternal rest
in a London night: My friend on the road to Syria,
we haven't reached Syria yet, don't hurry, don't make the jasmine
a bereaved mother, or test me with an elegy:
how do I lift the poem's burden off you and me?

> The poem of those who don't love describing fog
> is his poem.
> The coat of the clouds over the church
> is his coat.
> The secret of two hearts seeking Barada
> is his secret.
> The palm tree of the Sumerian woman, mother of song,
> is his tree.
> And the keys of Córdoba in the south of fog
> are his keys.
> He doesn't append his name to his poems,
> the little girl knows him
> if she feels the pinpricks
> and the salt in her blood.
> He, like me, is haunted by his heart,
> and I, like him, don't append my will to my name.
> And the wind knows my folks' new address
> on the slopes of an abyss
> in the south of the distant …

Farewell, my friend, farewell, and bid Syria salaam.
I am no longer young to carry myself
upon the words, no longer young
to finish this poem …

And at night I walk with the *Dhad*, my private language, I walk
with the night in the *Dhad*, an old man urging
an aging horse to fly to the Eiffel Tower: O my language,
help me to adapt and embrace the universe. Inside me
there's a balcony no one passes under for a greeting.
And outside me a world that doesn't return the greeting.
My language, will I become what you'll become, or are you
what becomes of me? Teach me the wedding parade
that merges the alphabet with my body parts.
Teach me to become a master not an echo.
And wrap me up in your wool, help me

to differ and reach consonance. Give birth to me and I
will give birth to you, sometimes I'm your son, and other times
your father and mother. If you are, I am. If I am, you are.
Call this new time by its foreign names, and host
the distant stranger and life's simple prose
for my poetry to mature. For who, if I utter what isn't poetry,
will understand me? Who will speak to me of a hidden
longing for a lost time if I utter what isn't poetry?
And who will know the stranger's land? …

The night became tranquil and complete, a flower
woke up and breathed by the garden fence.

I said to myself: I am witness that I'm still alive
even if from afar. And that I dreamt about the one who had been
dreaming, like me, I dreamt he was I and not another …
and that my day, Tuesday, was long and spacious,
and that my night was brief like a short act appended
to a play after the curtains had come down.
Still I won't harm anyone
if I add: It was a beautiful day,
like a true love story aboard an express train.

> If the canary doesn't sing,
> my friend,
> blame only yourself.
> If the canary doesn't sing
> to you, my friend,
> then sing to it … sing to it.

Hoopoe

Mahmoud Darwish

Translation by Fady Joudah

We haven't approached the land of our distant star yet. The poem takes us
through the needle's eye to weave, for space, the aba of the new horizon.
We are captives. Even if our wheat leapt off the fence and the swallow burst
out of our broken chains, captives, what we are, what we love and want ...
But there is a hoopoe within us who dictates his letters to the olive of exile.
Our letters came back to us from our letters, to write anew
what the rain writes of primitive flowers on the stone of distance.
And the journey—the echo travels from and to us. We aren't basil
to return in spring to our little windows. We aren't leaves
for the wind to take us to our coasts. Here or there is a clear line
for wandering. How many years must we raise our dead
as mirrors to the sweet mysterious? How many times
must the wounded carry mountains of salt to find the commandments?
Our letters came back to us from our letters. Here or there is a clear line—
for shadow. How many seas must we cross inside the desert?
How many tablets must we forget?
How many prophets must we kill at noon?
How many nations must we resemble to become—
a tribe? This road, our road, is the reed upon the words that darn the hem
of the aba between our desolation and the earth, and the earth distances itself
to doze off in our saffron sunset. So let's open
like a palm and lift our time to the gods ...
I am a hoopoe—the guide told the master of things—I search for a lost sky.
We said: What remains of the wilderness is only what the wilderness finds
of us: the remnants of skin over thorn, the warrior's song to home, and the mouth
of space. Our relics are in front of us. And behind us is absurdity's shell ...
I am a hoopoe—the guide told us—then flew with the rays and the dust.
Then our sages asked about the meaning of story and departure:
Where did we come from when our relics are in front of us,
and the willows behind us? From our names we come
to our names, and we hide forgetfulness from our kids. The stags spring from stags

CREDIT: Darwish, Mahmoud. 2009. "The Hoopoe." Pp. 42-154 in *If I Were Another* by Mahmoud Darwish. Translation from the Arabic by Fady Joudah. New York: Farrar, Straus and Giroux. Gratefully reprinted by permission from the publisher of the poem.

onto the temples. And the birds lay eggs over the comedy of statues. We didn't ask
why humans weren't born of trees that permit return. The oracles told us
the hearts are weighed on a scale in ancient Egypt. The oracles told us
the obelisk supports the horizon from falling onto the ages. And that we
will repeat our journey there on the outer darkness. And the oracles told us
the kings are our judges, and the witnesses are our foes. And the soul
is guarded by shepherds. Our journey is a bridge between two rivers,
and we weren't born to be erased, though life obliterates …
I am a hoopoe—the guide said—I will be guided to the spring if vegetation dries.
We said: We aren't birds. He said: You won't reach Him, all is His,
and all is within Him, He's in everything, search for Him if you want to find Him,
He is within Him. We said: We aren't birds to fly. He said: My wings are my time,
and passion is passion's fire, so burn to cast the place's body off yourselves.
We said: Did you return from Sheba to take us to a new Sheba? Our letters
came back to us from our letters but you didn't return … you didn't.
And in Greece you didn't comprehend Aristophanes,
didn't find the city in the city. You didn't
find the house of compassion to wrap us up in the silk of serenity.
You didn't attain the meaning, so the poets' obsession enchanted you: "Fly,
daughters of my feathers, birds of the plains and wadis, fly
swiftly fly toward my wings and toward my voice." There is a yearning
in us to fly in our passions, but humans aren't birds to fly …
Hoopoe of words, when you hatch the meaning and the birds
snatch us from language, son of strain, when the butterfly
splits from its elements and feeling resides it, dissolve our clay,
for the light to cleave the image of things. Soar and clarify
the distance between what we were and what will be our final present.
We move away, but end up near our truth and the walls of our estrangement.
Passage is our obsession. We're the duality of earth-sky, sky-earth
and around us are fence and fence. So what's behind the fence?
Adam was taught all the names for the grand secret to bloom,
and the secret is our journey to the secretive. Humans are birds that don't fly …
I am a hoopoe—the guide said—and below us is Noah's flood. Babylon.
Petrified remains. The vapor of the nations' call to water.
Skeletons and an end like a beginning to an end.
We said: Soar, for the murderer to forget his victims.
Soar above us. Soar for the creator to forget his creation, his things,
and the names in the myth of creation that we exchange.
—Did you know all this beforehand, hoopoe?
—I knew that a volcano would draw the new image of the universe.
—Yet you, postman of the earth, said nothing. —I tried … We know
there are enough ghosts in the hoopoe to make him search in the graveyards
for his beloved … he had a mother, and a south that settles on his flight.
He had the myth of speculation that is crowned with water … and among his paths
there are a king and a woman … and an army guarding the two juvenile bodies
from our dreams.
We have enough of the desert

to grant the hoopoe the rein to our mirage and clouds.
We have enough fragility to hand over to him our sleep's sleep.
Take us, hoopoe, our tongues are puzzled, how do we praise
the One who asked for praise when His praise is within Him.
All is within Him for all. We accepted that
we are humans in this desert, and we dissolved into love. Where
is our palm tree so we'll find our hearts in the dates?
And God is more beautiful than the road to God. But those who travel
don't return from a wandering to be lost in another wandering!
They know the road is the arrival at the beginning of the impossible road.
Hoopoe of secrets, struggle for us to witness our love in the beloved.
It's an eternal journey, this search for the adjective of the One who has no
adjective. His adjectives are free from our description and His traits. Take us high.
What remains of us is our journey to Him. To Him
we plead what we endure in departure …
Our blood is His nations' wine over the marble and on the supper table.
Hoopoe, "There is no you but you," so steal us to you if you please, and guide us
one day to the quick earth, before we spin in the bottomless pit, guide us
one day to trees we were secretly born under to hide our shadow,
guide us to childhood. To doves that once faked what they were to disgrace us.
The children grew up but didn't fly like the doves. How we wish. We wish. Perhaps
we'll fly one day … humans are birds that don't fly. And the earth
is larger when we're ignorant, smaller when we know our ignorance.
But we're the descendants of this clay, and the devil of fire tries, as we do,
to attain the nearby secrets, to burn us and burn our minds.
Yet the mind is only smoke, let it get lost! The hearts will guide us.
So take us, hoopoe of secrets, to our vanishing through His vanishing.
Take us high then bring us down to bid our mother farewell.
Endlessly waiting for our horses, she wants to die when light breaks, or live
for Nishapur as a widow who adorns our nights.
She "wants only God from God" … take us then!
Love is not to attain the beloved, the hoopoe said:
On a flute's echo a lover sent the mare of absence
for his woman and abridged the road and said: I am she. And she
is the "I" unraveling from despair toward hope, to return me to despair.
And my roads to her doors are endless … and my "I" flew "so the only I is I …"
And the nations' roads to the same old springs are endless!
We said: The canons will become complete
when we get past this archipelago and free the captives from the tablets.
Let the void sit in its arcade so the human in us can complete the migration …
Who are these flutes looking for in the forests? We are the strangers.
We are the folk of the abandoned temple, abandoned atop our white horses—
the reed sprouts over us and meteors flash above us, we search for our final station.
There's no earth left where we haven't built an exile for our small tent.
Are we the skin of the earth? Who are the words looking for inside us?
Are these the words that brought us to the court of vision in the underworld?
The words that built the temples to tame its desolate beast with image and psalm?

Our relics are in front of us. And behind us. Here and there. And the oracles
told us: The city worships the ancestors in ancient China. The oracles told us:
The ancestors take their throne to the holy grave—they take
the girls as wives and the war captives as guards. The oracles told us:
Divinity is the twin of man in ancient India. The oracles told us
what the creatures told us: "You are also who He is" … although we didn't
raise our fig tree for the comers from the south to hang us on it.
Are we the skin of the earth? We used to bite the rock and open—
a space for the jasmine. We used to seek refuge in God from his guards and wars.
We used to believe what we learned of the words. Poetry used to descend—
from the fruits of our nights, and lead our goats to the pastures on the raisin trail.
The dawn was blue, soft, and moist. And when we dreamt we used to be content
with the borders of our houses: we would see honey on the honeycomb, then
gather it, see the square of a sesame seed complete in our sleep, then sift it, see
what we would see at dawn. Dream was the lover's handkerchief.
But we didn't raise our fig tree for the comers from the south to hang us on it.
I am a hoopoe—the guide replied—then flew … and the words flew—
from us. The Flood came before us. We didn't take off the clothes of the earth—
the Flood came before us. We hadn't begun the self wars yet. It came before us.
We hadn't harvested the barley of our yellow fields. It came before us.
We hadn't burnished our stones with a ram's horn, the Flood
came before us. We hadn't despaired of apples. The sad mother would bear
brothers from our flesh, not from the chestnut trunk, nor
from iron. The sad mother would bear brothers to erect the exile
of anthem. The sad mother would bear brothers to dwell
in the palm fronds, if they want, or on the plains of our horses. And she would bear
brothers who anoint Abel king of the throne of dust.
But our journey to forgetfulness has turned long. And the veil ahead of us masks
the veil. Perhaps the mid-road is the road to a road of clouds.
Perhaps we are, hoopoe of secrets, ghosts searching for ruins?
The hoopoe said: Leave your bodies and follow me, leave the earth—the mirage
and follow me. And leave your names. Don't ask me for an answer.
The answer is the road and the only road is to vanish in the fog.
We asked: Are you under the spell of al-Attar?
—He spoke to me then went into the belly of Passion's Wadi.
We asked: Did al-Ma'arri stop by the Wadi of Knowledge?
—His road is the absurd. We asked: And Ibn Sina … did he answer
your question and did he see you? —I see through the heart, not through
philosophy. Are you a Sufi then? —I am a hoopoe. I have no want. "I want
not to want" … then the hoopoe disappeared into yearning: O love,
you have tormented us. From travel to travel you send us in vain. You have
tormented us and estranged us from our kin, from our water and air. You have
corrupted us. Emptied the hours of sunset from the sunset. Dispossessed us
of our first words. Robbed the peach tree of our days, dispossessed our days. O love,
you have tormented us, and robbed us. Estranged us from all things and veiled
yourself with autumn leaves. You have robbed us, love. Left not a little
thing for us to search for you in it, or to kiss its shadow, so leave

for us an ear of wheat within the soul that loves you more. Don't break the glass
of the universe around our calling. Don't fret. Don't clamor. Be calm
for a while so we can see the elements in you as they lift their total wedding
toward you. Approach us so we can realize for once: Do we deserve
to be the slaves of your hidden shudder? Don't scatter
what remains of our sky's rubble. O love, you have tormented us,
O gift, you have dispersed us to guide our unknown toward rising …
this unknown is not ours and the river's mouth is not ours,
and life rises before us like leaves of ancient cypress, to lead
longing toward longing. You have tormented us, love, made us absent
from ourselves, and dispossessed our names …
Then, intoxicated, the hoopoe reappeared and said: Fly just to fly.
We said: We're only lovers. We have tired of the whiteness of love, we long
for a mother, a dry land, and a parent. Are we who we were and who we'll be?
He said: Unite on every path and vaporize to reach the One
whom the senses cannot reach. Each heart
is a universe of secrets. Fly just to fly. We said: We are only lovers,
we have often died and been elated. We are only lovers. Longing
is exile. Our love is exile. And our wine is exile. And exile
is the history of this heart. We have often said to the scent of the place: Petrify
so we can sleep. We have often told the trees of the place to strip off
the ornament of invasions so we can find the place.
And non-place is the place when its soul becomes remote from its history …
Exile is the soul that distances us from our land, toward the beloved.
Exile is the land that distances us from our soul, toward the stranger.
No sword remains that hasn't sheathed itself in our flesh.
And our enemy-brothers saddled the enemy's horses to exit our dreams.
The past is exile: we plucked the plums of our joy off the barren summer.
Thoughts are exile: we watched tomorrow beneath the windows then broke through
our present's walls to reach it, but it became the past in a soldier's ancient shield.
And poetry is exile when we dream then forget where we were when we waken.
Do we deserve a gazelle? Hoopoe of secrets,
take us to our endless tomorrow! Hang our time over the vastness. Take us high.
All of nature is soul, and the earth appears from here
like a breast for the grand shudder, and the horses of wind are our vessel …
So birds, O birds, fly just to fly, all of nature is soul. And encircle
your fascination with the yellow hand, your sun, and dissolve. Then turn around
after you've burned, and head toward the land, your land,
to illuminate the tunnel of the solid question about this existence and about
the little wall of time. All of nature is soul, and soul is the body's last dance.
Fly higher than flight … higher than your sky … just to fly higher
than the grand love … than the sacred … than the divine and the sensuous.
Liberate yourself from all the wings of questions about beginning and destiny.
The universe is smaller than a butterfly's wing in the courtyard of the large heart.
In a grain of wheat we met, then parted in bread and in the journey.
Who are we in this anthem that we should roof the desert with this copious rain?
Who are we in this anthem that we should free the living

from the captivity of graves? Fly with your swift wings, birds, on squalls of silk.
You may fly as our elation. The universal echo will call to you: Fly
to attain the flash of vision. But we will descend onto ourselves,
and if we waken, we will return to visit a time that wasn't enough
for our happiness or for the climate of Resurrection.
Who are we in this anthem that we should meet its antithesis as a door to a wall?
And what good is our idea without humans
since we are now made of fire and light?
I am a hoopoe, the guide replied. And we said: We are a flock of birds, words
are fed up with us and we with them, we're full of thirst, and echo has scattered us.
For how much longer will we fly? The drunkard hoopoe said: Our goal is the vastness.
We said: And what's behind it? He said: Vastness after vastness after vastness.
We said: We're tired. He said: You won't find a pine tree to rest on. What
you ask of descent is in vain, so soar just to soar. We said: How about tomorrow,
we'll fly again tomorrow … the earth will still be there, a ripened breast suckled
by the clouds, a gold that scratches the blue shudder around our homes. The earth
has everything—even if we don't know it. We shall return when we return
to see it with our hoopoe's eyes that have possessed our eyes.
Salaam upon the earth, salaam unto it …
It has the bed of the universe with cotton sheets made of vision and clouds.
It sleeps on arms of water as owner of its image and ours. And it has
a small moon that combs its shadow like a servant. And the moon passes
among our hearts frightened of exile and of the fate of myth,
then darkness illuminates it like a vigil for the state of the self near the miracles.
Is this what words are born out of, for clay
to become man? Did we know the earth to forget it and forget
the fish of childhood around its navel? Do we see from afar what we don't see
when near? The days were often our fortresses on the string of language.
The rivers were often our flutes though we didn't notice. And the marble
often imprisoned some of our angels but we never knew it. And Egypt and Syria
have often lost their way. There's a land to the land
above which our hoopoe was captive. There's a soul to the land—
the wind scattered it. And Noah didn't leave all the messages for us.
Christ walked to Galilee and the wounds in us clapped. Here, the doves
are the words of our dead. Here, the Babylonian ruins
are a mole in our journey's armpit.
Here an apple body swims in the galaxy.
And water is that body's belt as it flows along eternity,
embodied in our eulogies, and then returns to itself
like a mother who covers us with her naked fur of longing, hides what we've done
to the lung and the fire of her rose, hides our journey's war, and what the sword
has done to the map of grass around the shores of the sacred feathers.
Our mother is our mother. The Athenians' mother.
The ancient Persians' mother. Plato's, Zaradasht's, Plotinus's,
Suhrwardi's, and everyone's mother. Each child is a master in his mother.
The beginning and end are hers. As if she is what she desires to be: birth.
And if she desires, she is also the forbidden death.

You fed and nourished us, mother, to feed our children, so when is the weaning?
O spider of love. Death is a murder. We love you, O how we love you,
grant us mercy. Don't kill us a second time and don't give birth to the serpents
near the Tigris … and let us walk on the gazelles of your waist
near your waist, the air is the dwelling place.
Lure us as the mischievous partridge is lured to the nets, and embrace us.
Were you there before our migration?
The passion of wandering changes us into a poem
that has opened its windows for the pigeons to complete the poem
then carry it as a meaning that brings back the sap to the invisible
trees on the banks of our souls …
Fly, then, just to fly in the courtyards of this heart, fly.
What good is our idea without the human …
since we are made of clay and light?
Did you know, hoopoe, what crown was on your head?
The hoopoe replied: My mother's grave. When I fly carrying secrets and news,
my mother is a festival on my head …
He's a hoopoe, we said, he's the guide and what's in him is in us, hung by time
like a bell for the wadis. Yet the place becomes narrow in vision and time breaks.
What do you see, hoopoe … what do you see in the faraway image of shadow?
—I see the shadow of His image over us, so let's soar to see Him, He is the only He:
"O heart … my mother and sister," my wife, pour yourself out to see Him …
But after all, our hoopoe, we said, is just a hoopoe …
Water has a throne that rises beneath the drought, and the holm oaks rise also.
Water has the color of the field when the zephyr of dawn lifts it on the horses' backs.
Water has the taste of the gift of song lunging from memory's garden.
Water has the scent of the beloved on the marble, increasing our thirst and stupor.
And our hoopoe has horses of water that rise under his drought as the scepter rises.Water
has the shape of sunrise's brevity when it splits us in two: human and bird.
And our hoopoe . . . has a time he once carried, and he once had a tongue.
And our hoopoe . . . has a land he once carried as messages to the distant heavens.
There's no religion the hoopoe hasn't offered to the creatures as a departure to God.
There's no love that hasn't tormented the hoopoe
with breaking through a lover to his other.
And the hoopoe is always a traveler.
Who are you in this anthem? I am the guide, he said.
And the hoopoe is always a traveler. Who are you in this anthem?
I am departure, he said. "O heart . . . my mother and sister," pour yourself out
so the impossible can see you—and for you to see it,
and take me, both of you, to my final mirror. Our hoopoe said this then flew . . .
Are we what we were? There are trees on our ruins and a beautiful moon
in our travel. And we have a life over there in others' lives.
Yet we were coerced into the orphaned Samarkand.
We don't have a king to bring back. The days left
to us what the flute bequeathed of the days . . . the nearest of them is farthest.
And we have of rain what the lablab ivy has.
We are now what we were, we have come back

coerced to the myths that didn't expand for our arrival, and we organize
our days around our anthem. And we have temples over there, and here
we have a god whose martyrs praise.
And we have flowers of night musk the day shuts out.
And we have a life in others' lives. We have oil and wheat—
we didn't make our tent out of our willows, we didn't make gods
out of sulfur for the soldiers to come and worship. We found everything
ready: our broken names in the jars
of clay . . . our women's tears of old berry stains
on the garments . . . our old hunting rifles . . . and a previous festival
we can't retrieve. The wasteland is packed with traces of human absence.
And it seems we were here once. It seems
there are enough tools here to pitch a tent above the wind.
And the Flood has no tattoos on the wrinkles of the mountain with green borders.
But there are a thousand nations in us that have passed between song and spear.
We came to learn that we came to return from an absence we don't desire.
And we have a life we haven't yet tried.
And an immortal salt that hasn't immortalized who we are.
And we have steps no one before us has taken . . . so fly,
fly, O birds, in the courtyards of this heart, fly,
and gather around our hoopoe, and fly . . . just . . . to fly!

A River Dies of Thirst: Journals
by Mahmoud Darwish
Translations from the Arabic by Catherine Cobham

New York: Archipelago Books
Publication Date: September 2009
160 pages
ISBN-10: 0981955711
ISBN-13: 978-0981955711

"This remarkable collection of Mahmoud Darwish's poems and prose meditations is both lyrical and philosophical, questioning and wise, full of irony and protest and play. "Every beautiful poem is an act of resistance." As always, Darwish's musings on unrest and loss dwell on love and humanity; myth and dream are inseparable from truth. "Truth is plain as day." Throughout the book, Darwish returns frequently to his ongoing and often lighthearted conversation with death. Catherine Cobham teaches Arabic language and literature at St Andrews University, Scotland, and has translated a number of Arab authors, including Naguib Mahfouz, Yusuf Idris, Fuad al-Takarli, Hanan al-Shaykh and Liana Badr."—Publisher

A River Dies of Thirst

Mahmoud Darwish

Translation by Catherine Cobham

A river was here
and it had two banks
and a heavenly mother who nursed it on drops from the clouds
A small river moving slowly
descending from the mountain peaks
visiting villages and tents like a charming lively guest
bringing oleander trees and date palms to the valley
and laughing to the nocturnal revellers on its banks:
'Drink the milk of the clouds
and water the horses
and fly to Jerusalem and Damascus'
Sometimes it sang heroically
at others passionately
It was a river with two banks
and a heavenly mother who nursed it on drops from the clouds
But they kidnapped its mother
so it ran short of water
and died, slowly, of thirst.

CREDIT: Darwish, Mahmoud. 2009. "A River Dies of Thirst." Pp. 36 in *A River Dies of Thirst: Journals* by Mahmoud Darwish. Translated from the Arabic by Catherine Cobham. Brooklyn, NY: Archipelago Books. Gratefully reprinted by permission from the publisher of the poem.

Assassination

Mahmoud Darwish

Translation by Catherine Cobham

The critics kill me sometimes:
they want a particular poem
a particular metaphor
and if I stray up a side road
they say: 'He has betrayed the road'
And if I find eloquence in grass
they say: 'He has abandoned the steadfastness of the holm oak'
And if I see the rose in spring as yellow
they ask: 'Where is the blood of the homeland in its petals?'
And if I write: 'It is the butterfly my youngest sister
at the garden door'
they stir the meaning with a soup spoon
And if I whisper: 'A mother is a mother, when she loses her child
she withers and dries up like a stick'
they say: 'She trills with joy and dances at his funeral
for his funeral is his wedding'

And if I look up at the sky to see
the unseen
they say: 'Poetry has strayed far from its objectives'
The critics kill me sometimes
and I escape from their reading
and thank them for their misunderstanding
then search for my new poem.
River Dies.

CREDIT: Darwish, Mahmoud. 2009. "Assassination." Pp. 51-52 in *A River Dies of Thirst: Journals* by Mahmoud Darwish. Translated from the Arabic by Catherine Cobham. Brooklyn, NY: Archipelago Books. Gratefully reprinted by permission from the publisher of the poem.

Nero

Mahmoud Darwish

Translation by Catherine Cobham

What's going on in Nero's mind as he watches Lebanon burn? His eyes wander ecstatically and he walks like someone dancing at a wedding: This madness is my madness, I know best, so let them set light to everything beyond my control. And the children have to learn to behave themselves and stop shouting when I'm playing my tunes!

And what's going on in Nero's mind as he watches Iraq burn? Does it please him that he awakens a memory in the history of the jungle that preserves his name as an enemy of Hamurabbi and Gilgamesh and Abu Nuwas: My law is the mother of all laws, the flower of eternity grows in my fields, and poetry – what does that mean?

And what goes on in Nero's mind as he watches Palestine burn? Does it delight him that his name is recorded in the roll of prophets as a prophet that nobody's ever believed in before? As a prophet of killing who God entrusted with correcting the countless mistakes in the heavenly books: I too am God's mouthpiece!

And what goes on in Nero's mind as he watches the world burn? I am master of the Day of Judgement. Then he orders the camera to stop rolling, because he doesn't want anyone to see that his fingers are on fire at the end of this long American movie!

CREDIT: Darwish, Mahmoud. 2009. "Nero." Pp. 9 in *A River Dies of Thirst: Journals* by Mahmoud Darwish. Translated from the Arabic by Catherine Cobham. Brooklyn, NY: Archipelago Books. Gratefully reprinted by permission from the publisher of the poem.

The Enemy

Mahmoud Darwish

Translation by Catherine Cobham

I was there a month ago. I was there a year ago. I was always there as if I was never anywhere else. In 1982 the same thing happened to us as is happening now. We were besieged and killed and fought against the hell we encountered. The casualties / martyrs don't resemble one another. Each of them has a distinctive physique and distinctive features, different eyes and a different name and age. The killers are the ones who all look the same. They are one being, distributed over different pieces of hardware, pressing electronic buttons, killing and vanishing. He sees us but we don't see him, not because he's a ghost but because he's a steel mask on an idea—he is featureless, eyeless, ageless and nameless. It is he who has chosen to have a single name: the enemy.

CREDIT: Darwish, Mahmoud. 2009. "The Enemy." Pp. 8 in *A River Dies of Thirst: Journals* by Mahmoud Darwish. Translated from the Arabic by Catherine Cobham. Brooklyn, NY: Archipelago Books. Gratefully reprinted by permission from the publisher of the poem.

The House as Casualty

Mahmoud Darwish

Translation by Catherine Cobham

In one minute the entire life of a house is ended. The house as casualty is also mass murder, even if it is empty of its inhabitants. A mass grave of raw materials intended to build a structure with meaning, or a poem with no importance in time of war. The house as casualty is the severance of things from their relationships and from the names of feelings, and from the need of tragedy to direct its eloquence at seeing into the life of the object. In every object there is a being in pain – a memory of fingers, of a smell, an image. And houses are killed just like their inhabitants. And the memory of objects is killed: stone, wood, glass, iron, cement are scattered in broken fragments like living beings. And cotton, silk, linen, papers, books are torn to pieces like proscribed words. Plates, spoons, toys, records, taps, pipes, door handles, fridges, washing machines, flower vases, jars of olives and pickles, tinned food all break just like their owners. Salt, sugar, spices, boxes of matches, pills, contraceptives, antidepressants, strings of garlic, onions, tomatoes, dried okra, rice and lentils are crushed to pieces just like their owners. Rent agreements, marriage documents, birth certificates, water and electricity bills, identity cards, passports, love letters are torn to shreds like their owners' hearts. Photographs, toothbrushes, combs, cosmetics, shoes, underwear, sheets, towels fly in every direction like family secrets broadcast aloud in the devastation. All these things are a memory of the people who no longer have them and of the objects that no longer have the people—destroyed in a minute. Our things die like us, but they aren't buried with us.

CREDIT: Darwish, Mahmoud. 2009. "The House As Casualty." Pp. 12 in *A River Dies of Thirst: Journals* by Mahmoud Darwish. Translated from the Arabic by Catherine Cobham. Brooklyn, NY: Archipelago Books. Gratefully reprinted by permission from the publisher of the poem.

The Rest of A Life

Mahmoud Darwish

Translations by Catherine Cobham

If someone said to me: 'You're going to die here this evening
so what will you do in the time that remains?' I would say
'I will look at my watch
drink a glass of juice
and crunch on an apple
and observe at length an ant that has found her day's supply of food
Then look at my watch:
there is still time to shave
and take a long shower. A thought will occur to me:
One should look nice to write
so I'll wear something blue
I will sit until noon, alive, at my desk
not seeing a trace of colour in the words
white, white, white

I will prepare my last meal
pour wine into two glasses: for me
and an unexpected guest
then take a nap between two dreams
but the sound of my snoring will wake me
Then I will look at my watch:
there is still time to read
I will read a canto of Dante and half a *mu'allaqa*
and see how my life goes from me
into other people, and not wonder who
will take its place'
'Just like that?'
'Just like that'
'Then what?'

CREDIT: Darwish, Mahmoud. 2009. "The Rest of A Life." Pp. 19-20 in *A River Dies of Thirst: Journals* by Mahmoud Darwish. Translated from the Arabic by Catherine Cobham. Brooklyn, NY: Archipelago Books. Gratefully reprinted by permission from the publisher of the poem.

'I will comb my hair
and throw the poem, this poem
in the rubbish bin
put on the latest shirt from Italy
say my final farewell to myself with a backing of Spanish violins
then
walk
to the graveyard!'

If We Want To

Mahmoud Darwish

Translation by Catherine Cobham

We will become a people, if we want to, when we learn that we are not angels, and that evil is not the prerogative of others

We will become a people when we stop reciting a prayer of thanksgiving to the sacred nation every time a poor man finds something to eat for his dinner

We will become a people when we can sniff out the sultan's gatekeeper and the sultan without a trial

We will become a people when a poet writes an erotic description of a dancer's belly

We will become a people when we forget what the tribe tells us, when the individual recognises the importance of small details

We will become a people when a writer can look up at the stars without saying: 'Our country is loftier and more beautiful!'

We will become a people when the morality police protect a prostitute from being beaten up in the streets

We will become a people when the Palestinian only remembers his flag on the football pitch, at camel races, and on the day of the Nakba

We will become a people, if we want to, when the singer is allowed to chant a verse of Surat al-Rahman at a mixed wedding reception

We will become a people when we respect the right, and the wrong.

CREDIT: Darwish, Mahmoud. 2009. "If We Want To." Pp. 42-43 in *A River Dies of Thirst: Journals* by Mahmoud Darwish. Translated from the Arabic by Catherine Cobham. Brooklyn, NY: Archipelago Books. Gratefully reprinted by permission from the publisher of the poem.

Selected Poems

Country • Practicing Loving Kindness • Peace • No • Night Sky • Living History • Cyclones and Seeds

Lisa Suhair Majaj

Palestinian-American Writer, Scholar and Poet

---

lmajaj@cytanet.com.cy

This is a selected offering of new and previously published poems by Palestinian-American writer, scholar, and poet Lisa Suhair Majaj. She writes, "poetry emerges from the self, but is grounded in the wider world. As poets, we write in the hope that words can weave a cord of connection between individuals, between cultures, between countries—that words can take us beyond our single selves and locate us within the web of humanity. We all wish to be 'candles in the darkness'—we write in the hope that our words may help to buoy others on their journeys through personal and public histories, just as the words of Darwish have buoyed, and still buoy, so many of us. We too often experience ourselves as small boats bobbing in a large sea of indifference and injustice, but connected by words we remember our humanity—our place in the whole. And out of this connection we find the power to bear witness and to take action, aware that the whole is larger than any sum of its parts, and that the smallest gesture resonates beyond our knowing." The long poem "Country" is published here for the first time. Poem "Cyclones and Seeds" was first published in *Mizna*, Volume 4, Issue 1, 2002, p. 15-20. Poem "No" was first published in *Nerve: Linking Artists, Activists, Poets, Thinkers, Creative Folks and Community*, Issue #1, Power and Choice (Summer 2006). Poem "Living in History" was first published in *The Other Voices International Project*, Vol. 18, Feb. 2006. Poem "Practicing Loving Kindness" was first published in *Cadences: A Journal of Literature and the Arts in Cyprus*, vol. 2, # 1&2, summer 2006. Poem "Night Sky" was first published in *Babel Fruit*, Volume 3 Issue 4, Autumn 2008, online at *http://web.mac.com/renkat/BABEL_FRUIT/BabelFruit.html*.

Lisa Suhair Majaj, a Palestinian-American writer and scholar, has read and published her work widely across the U.S., Europe and the Middle East. Her poetry and creative nonfiction have appeared in journals such as *World Literature Today, 91st Meridian, Perhihelion Review, Banipal: Magazine of Modern Arab Literature, South Atlantic Quarterly, Visions International, Cadences: A Journal of Literature and the Arts in Cyprus, The Jerusalem Times* and elsewhere. She is also a longtime scholar of Arab-American literature. Her previous book publications include two chapbooks of poetry and three co-edited collections of literary essays: *Intersections: Gender, Nation and Community in Arab Women's Novels, Etel Adnan: Critical Essays on the Arab-American Writer and Artist,* and *Going Global: The Transnational Reception of Third World Women Writers.* Her academic affiliations have included Amherst College, College of the Holy Cross and Northeastern University. She recently won the Del Sol Press Poetry Prize for her poetry volume *Geographies of Light.* She lives in Nicosia, Cyprus.

COUNTRY

Here there are cypress trees
tall enough to break through fear
green as the promise to keep on living

here we are far away, and near

> cordon of gasps
> breath flung in horror
> hauling in grief
>
> stunned faces tilted upwards
> too dazed to cry

broken phone lines
endless dialing
        paroxysm of fear
till we reach those there

voices broken by static

> oh safe!
>   train late
>   meeting cancelled
>   child sick
> but for a trick of fate
> would have been
>   there

country of agony
       country of fear

• • •

James Wang, 21, a photography student...
looked up and saw people high in the north tower...
'They jumped. One woman, her dress
was billowing out.' —New York Times, Sept. 13, 2001

they threw themselves headfirst
into the dark morning

some holding hands
others swimming singly downwards
minnows
caught in the cascade
of vertical fire
carried on the downdraft
a short time

• • •

"This is America," a man said. "How can it happen in America? How?
—New York Times, Sept. 13, 2001

no words for the suddenly empty skyline

smoke hangs over history
        ash blackening lungs

those crushed   burned
killed in a desperate leap into

                        nothing

their absence a fierce wound
borne
by the living

walls plastered with pleas for the disappeared

        looking for
                Lydia, 21, birthmark on her left cheek
            Robert, last seen on the 21st floor
        Mary, brown hair, black eyes
                Tom, walks with a limp

    grimed anguish
    flapping in the rain

• • •

beneath the news
smolder embers of history

with blurred vision, we peer into the dark
of America

> *Here is a map of our country:*
> *here is the Sea of Indifference, glazed with salt…*
> *A patriot is one who wrestles for the*
> *   soul of her country*
> *as she wrestles for her own being…A patriot is a citizen trying to wake*
> *from the burnt-out dream of innocence…to remember…*
> *that every flag that flies today is a cry of pain"*
> *   (Adrienne Rich, An Atlas of the Difficult World)*

at the nation's borders
the desperate peer across rivers
          deep as grief
          wide as history

tributaries bridged by the reaching hands
of children

          ravines filled with sharp rocks, shrapnel,
          ravaged bodies, blackened earth

• • •

we built tall buildings
that did not make us large

now we are puny
afraid to fly   travel   speak
to stand tall
               for justice

> *These are the places the U.S. has bombed since WWII: China. Korea.*
> *Guatemala. Indonesia. Cuba. The Belgian Congo. Peru. Laos.*
> *Vietnam. Cambodia. Grenada. Libya. El Salvador. Nicaragua.*
> *Panama. Iraq. Bosnia. Sudan. Yugoslavia. And now Afghanistan.*

If our bombs are large enough murderous enough
our planes swift enough
our guns big enough
our soldiers fierce enough
will we be unafraid?

(and what of the spirit
loud and angry
huddled inside its fear?)

• • •

if only sorrow could be pieced together
like the fragments of a broken bowl

each person a jagged shard
            in the whole

if only we could learn
                how large our hearts
        how fragile
• • •

half a million Iraqi children
cries stilled by hungry earth
graves dug by sanctions
by silence

in Afghanistan,
thousands bombed to
            nothingness
huts of mud and grass

a child in a hospital bed
wakes to limbless
orphan-hood

• • •

What have the trees seen?

        Every night the birds return to their nests
        perch on branches
        proffer insects to their young

        their little lives beyond us
        part of us

My heart, squeezed small,
        strains against its hard shell
    of grief

the children whose unknowing
              exploded in a fireball
                      of pain

the mothers
          who did not return,
      the fathers

(empty bellies,
long winter of starvation)
• • •

And if in my name bombs are dropped
on other women, other men,
children as precious as my own—
and I stay silent?
Grief is not enough.
Words are not enough.
Dollars are not enough.

And when one day my daughter asks,
where were you when children like me were dying?

• • •

What is the calculus of death?
How many small atrocities
equal one large atrocity?

> Altogether, at least 18 Palestinians were killed by the Israeli army
> in the past two days. Among those killed was a 71-year old man
> from Beit Likia, shot by soldiers for the crime of trying to bypass
> the earthen barrier blocking the single exit road from his village…
> another big-scale invasion by an armored column took place
> during the past day at the venerable town of Jericho, and there
> were sundry bombings and bombardments at various other spots.
> —Gush Shalom, Sept. 14, 2001

Palestinians distribute their children
among the neighbors,
in hopes that some, at least,
 will escape the shelling.

Another day,
another home demolition.

• • •

Sirens of mourning circle the world:
black band of sorrow.

Children in foreign countries hang plaques
on trees, remembering the New York dead.

Elsewhere, entire villages
are demolished, flushed out, cleansed.
Elected officials deny, excuse.

 (Did you flip quickly to the comics?
Was there even a story?)

• • •

              oh beautiful for

childhood mornings
                    overseas American

     I pledge allegiance to

hot dog Fridays Halloween dodgeball
library books shipped all the way
from the US of A

          my country 'tis

to Jordan land of   towel-heads
      terrorists
          camel jockeys
   halfbreeds

litany of unbelonging
          not American enough not white enough

litany of belonging
          who I was born as who my mother was who my children are

hand on my heart
          one nation,
                    indivisible

country of hatred
country of love

and to the republic
                    for which

and with belonging comes
responsibility

            with liberty and justice
                        for all

. . .

Generations do not cease to be born. And we are responsible to
them, because we are the only witnesses they have… the moment
we break faith with one another, the sea engulfs us, and the light
goes out. —Tim Wise, Alternet, Sept. 13, 200)

. . .

God bless
        America the beautiful
         America the good
            America the brave
          America the weapons merchant
        America the war-monger
                Fortress America
            America beacon of light and freedom
             America quencher of democracy
        America the righteous
            America sponsor of torturers, assassins, dictators
        America my country
                God bless

. . .

Oh Earth
                my world!

PRACTICING LOVING KINDNESS

Bless the maniac
barreling down the one-way street
the wrong way,
who shakes his fist when I honk.
May he live long enough
to take driving lessons.

Bless the postman
puffing under the no-smoking sign.
(When I complain, my mail
goes mysteriously missing
for months.) Bless all those
who debauch the air:
the mother wafting fumes
across her baby's carriage,
the man whose glowing stub
accosts a pregnant woman's face.
May they unlearn how to exhale.

Bless the politicians
who both give and receive
bribes and favors.
Bless the constituents
seeking personal gain,
the thieves, the liars, the sharks.
And bless the fools
who make corruption easy.
May they be spared
both wealth and penury.

Bless the soldiers guarding checkpoints
where women labor and give birth
in the dirt. Bless the settlers
swinging clubs into teenager's faces,
the boys shooting boys with bullets
aimed to kill, the men driving bulldozers
that flatten lives to rubble.
May they wake from the dream of power,
drenched in the cold sweat
of understanding. May they learn
the body's frailty, the immensity of the soul.

Bless the destroyers of Falluja,
the wreckers of Babylon,
the torturers of Abu Ghraib
and Guantanamo Bay.
May they understand desolation,
may they comprehend despair.

Bless the peace makers,
the teachers, the word-workers;
the wavers of flags
and the makers of fighter jets.
May we know the ends of our labor,
and the means. May we make
reparations. May we rebuild.

Bless this planet, so cudgeled,
so bounteous: the rain forests,
the tundra, the ozone layer.
May it persevere beyond
our human follies. May it bloom.

Bless cynicism. Bless hope.
Bless the fingers that type,
the computer that processes,
the printer that prints.
Bless email and snail mail.
Bless poetry books that cross oceans
in battered envelopes,
bearing small flames of words.

PEACE

Peace is two children walking toward each other from different sides of a barricade. Behind them are the tin shacks where they live with their parents in anger and desperation and loss. At the barricade they solemnly show each other what they have brought. One child has a shovel, the other child a watering can. Each has a seed. They dig the earth, plant the seeds, sprinkle water carefully, then go home. Each day they meet again at the barricade to see if the seeds have grown. When the first tiny shoots emerge they slap hands gleefully through the fence. When a bud emerges they laugh out loud. When a flower breaks to light, petals silken as sunshine, they go home humming a flower song, each in their own language.

No

There's no poetry in it,
but I need to say something about No,
how it stands up, no matter how unpopular,
in the face of injustice. Maybe it can't
thwart history: the powerful have always known
what they can do, and they do it.
No can't stop an avalanche.
But No could be a retaining wall
built of rough stones wrested from the earth,
carried one by one up the hill on someone's back.
No might be a tree in the middle of a village street:
traffic shifts to flow around it, its presence
a reminder of what used to be, what won't be
forgotten. No is the perimeter of stubborn cactus
springing up around destroyed villages.
You can bulldoze houses, evict or kill the inhabitants,
but the thorns of memory can't be eliminated.
No is steadfast. It knows what it's like
to have nothing in its hands but dignity.

NIGHT SKY

(Nicosia, Cyprus)

I line the candles up in my window:
tall, short, fat, round, square.
Lit, the flames burn equally.

Outside, the sky holds constellations
I remember from childhood nights,
my mother's patient voice

directing my gaze. Big Dipper.
Little Dipper. Hunter Orion's belt.
They shine unchanged

over this divided capital
on a divided island
in our divided world.

Candles and stars
are easier than news.
Television announcers describe

the infinite variety
of bombs. One flattens everything
in a two-kilometer radius:

libraries, movie theaters, schools.
Another sucks up acres of oxygen,
suffocating cats, cows, children.

From Baghdad, Barbara writes of families
so desperate to get a child out
they stop any foreigner in the street.

She pleads, "Just imagine our lives."
Tilting my head to the night sky
I watch the stars shine calmly

over our small world.
From wherever we are,
Baghdad is not so far.

LIVING IN HISTORY

It's true, whatever we do or don't do may come to haunt us.
Outside a man walks by: blue shirt, bald head. He blends
into the dusk, like the olive tree outside my window,
the blue-gray sky washed clean by recent rain,
the bird whose twittering heralds the evening.
May we all fit together like this: trees, birds, sky,
people, separate elements in a living portrait,
outlines smoothed by the forgiving wash
of lingering light. Whatever the skins we live in,
the names we choose, the gods we claim or disavow,
may we be like grains of sand on the beach at night:
a hundred million separate particles
creating a single expanse on which to lie back
and study the stars. And may we remember the generosity
of light: how it travels through unimaginable darkness,
age after age, to light our small human night.

CYCLONES AND SEEDS

Headlines declare retaliations,
military strikes. But in the lanes
kids bleed in the dust
while soldiers bar the way
to ambulances: no passage for mercy.

Love is in the details.
I want to know what that man,
twenty-five years old,
killed at his window
cradling his daughter in his arms,
ate for breakfast.
How many years of saving,
one dinar at a time,
it took to build that pile of rubble
that was once a home.
If the boy killed by a sniper
on his way to school
argued with his mother that morning.
If the pregnant woman shot at the checkpoint
was afraid of labor, anemic;
what she felt when her infant
turned beneath her heart.
What that stillborn child might have been named
if its desperate mother
had gotten through to the hospital
ringed with tanks.
Was it a girl? First born?
Fifth in a line of sons?

I want to save everything broken,
collect shards of crockery
from the rubble, gently blot the blood
from the gouged-up earth,
smooth the lashes that lie like tears
on the dead boys' cheeks.
I want to count the fingers and toes of each baby
before it's tucked into the earth.

I want the killers to look survivors in the eye
taste the gore of the dead in their mouths
lie down in the dirt with the corpses they've created
and remember their own history.
I want them to never sleep at night again.

I want the politicians brought before a line-up
of one Palestinian child one Israeli child one Afghani child
one American child one Iraqi child one British child
(all little girls, age four, with neat pigtails,
scrubbed faces, large trusting eyes).
Let them choose the child with the greatest value.

I want the headlines to scream
of Samer Suleiman Abu Mayaleh
fourteen years oldstripped
pushed face down in the street

      soldiers fired one bullet at close range
      up his rectum
      it burned through his body
      penetrating liver, heart
      blood soaking the dust
      from veins three quarters drained

they said a heart attack killed the boy

don't tell me you believe them
that you hadn't heard
that you're too busy to protest
that you couldn't do anything anyway
that the powers-that-be never listen

so what if we're shouting into a storm
if wind swallows words like rain
it takes just a single voice to break the silence

the world turns in the night
justice will not be silenced

voices planted in darkness
still spark the wounded earth to light

freedom is a seed   a plant   a prayer   a chant   a cyclone

it grows in hard places
courses through the bones
like light   a song   a sound a voice
a river of voices
bearing us forward

winged seeds upon the storm

Letter to Mahmoud Darwish

Amy Tighe

UMass and Boston College Alumni and Poet

artighe@aol.com

Abstract: The tradition of poets writing letters to other poets allows us to speak to each other in our own language. Amy Tighe, an emerging poet, responds to Mahmoud Darwish through a combination of her own experience of being friends with a Palestinian family, and her love of the intimacy of poetry.

March 31, 2009

Dear Mahmoud,

It's early spring March, and late in the afternoon, so the sunlight is sweetly desired, soft and decadent. Six o'clock, I feel as if the evening is still miles away, and sun beams stroke my keypad like a familiar cat. I have been trying to write to you for days, still thinking about what you said, how to reach you, how to reach me.

You are whole and dead, I am struggling, alive. This is the first time since I was a college kid that I have no money. The only resources are my words, and the paper I steal from the office. Twenty years ago, it was BIC pens, now it's access to the company printer and web mail. It solemns me, this lack of external resources, this closeness to an edge I used to think belonged to others, and I push myself to be able to listen. There are many times I feel I belong nowhere, so that this edge confronting me

makes me pay attention. You have now passed away; what do you want of me, still sickly alive? Why are there poems calling me to listen, to write, to call them "work"?

When my ex-husband, a freedom fighter I had known for decades, left me, I needed a roommate and so I advertised. I received a one line inquiry: "I am from Palestine, do you have a room for me?" As a divorced woman, hounded by the IRS, daughter of a German Jew and Irish immigrant, abandoned by a man who loved war more than me, I thought "in for a penny, in for a pound" and welcomed Abu Nour to my humble home. That has been one of the most comforting decisions I have ever made.

Abu Nour came as a scholar, with credentials and backing from an internationally renowned foundation; but more importantly, he came with a photo of his two-year-old daughter. In it, she is held tenderly by her mother and father as she reaches out for the camera—after all, she is

---

Amy Tighe is an emerging poet who has also performed as a storyteller locally as well as nationally. She is recently published as a poet, and appears at open mikes. She has studied the power of the spoken word in healing, through a five-year program on the Kabbalah as well as Native healing circles. Tighe is an accomplished businesswoman, and was one of the country's first LEED AP Realtors. She has been interviewed on NPR for her work as a green Realtor as well her work as a certified laughter coach. She loves the beach, and writing about how women heal war and how we can become more human through knowing the natural world. Tighe has a BA in Economics from UMass and MBA from Boston College.

two, and wants to hold it, and be the center there, too. At the precise moment when I accepted his security deposit, I was given an entirely a new vision, a grappling hook into a future we all can have, and one I never knew I would love so much.

To love someone from Palestine is to say to one's bones "do you mind changing your skeletal configuration, please?" The friends I always counted upon no longer liked me, my family thought I was staying depressed and traumatized from the divorce, and I no longer was asked to dinner. I have learned there are many hungers, and all of them demand their own deep questions. Your bones might reply, "We are not sure you are whole enough to ask this." And so your fundamental structure comes into war with itself.

Abu Nour cooks a dish called "upside down stew"—the closest thing to American food I can think of is Shepard's pie; but his is better and on cold New England nights, makes me wonder how anyone in the hot desolate desert of Palestine could dominate the winter so well. It even warms my nervous bones. This is a form of poetry, to me—comparing and sharing food.

In his first class in his Ph.D. program, a woman from Israel said "I did not come to America to sit next to the enemy." Abu Nour has spoken with respect to my cats, done the dishes twice without asking, never leaves the toilet seat up and I hate this woman immensely. Even woman to woman, I hate her. Eventually, however, she and Abu Nour become solid friends and teach others how to see each other as real beings, in a loving way. This is a form of poetry to me, when I can let it in, a new form of meeting through word.

It turns out, Mahmoud, that I am a person who knows war from the past. I guess this is different from knowing war from the present, and I am sorry, I don't understand that. But I know war and what it does to families, from the past. There are memories, and realities that have not settled in

the corners, not become annoying dust bunnies, or even rich ripe loam, from which a healthy future will flourish. They stay in the center, a blind elephant that I try to run from, to evenly escape all that I am, every day. When I visit Abu Nour's mother-in-law, the TV is chronically on, in Arabic, and the current catastrophes are parallel echoes I hear in my own memory.

Abu Nour reminds me of my first brother who died. He believes in the sanctity of life, the tender promise that actually breaking bread between two people can bring. Abu Nour is devout with his pita bread; my brother was an alter boy. I notice this in my roommate and I write for the first time in years—a rocky poem decrying a woman I don't know and hate. I mention bread as covenant and am unsure why.

Abu Nour focuses on his studies and his family. He seems to have one goal: love everyone enough to get his family here. In less than a month, he succeeds and rises to the top of his academic class, secures a place for his child and wife to live with him. They leave my home and start their own. I am proud and devastated. I take a poetry class for refuge. The teacher needs three poems to show I can write, and I throw whatever I have at her. She accepts me into her class and I am taken under the wings of baby boomers and early retirees. I have no money, a crazy job as a real estate agent and one grappling hook—this poetry class. And so I write.

Khalti, Abu Nour's mother-in-law, makes baba ganoosh, and to me it is an Iliad, complex and generous. She adds pomegranate seeds to her recipe, which I interpret as the blood of Christ in flesh that has been smoked by hand, and my poetry class blanches. Christ and eggplant are apparently not congruous with Cambridge poets. Two of my classmates are upper class women from minority backgrounds, and I think that surely they will network with me, a working class woman, a real estate agent, and help me get "THAT MILLION

DOLLAR SALE" which will give me the comfort to write more. But they don't. In class, they squabble over my use of words *"she spreads her branched thighs, against the barbed wire Israelis."* They leave me unanointed, unknown. I am not a peer, just a poet and they tell me I could be another Wallace Stevens, but don't hire me or refer me to their friends. I guess that is a compliment, or insult, I just can't tell. I feel left out.

Poetry is intimacy. It is an intimate act to write, to ask your senses to reveal their selves to you, to ask your self to listen to yourself and trust what your fingers are saying, what your calves are hearing, what your pancreas sighs over. It is an intimate act to ask someone to read what you have written, will they hear, will they dissolve the way you do when you write? Are your readers capable of osmosis? Are you? Am I?

I know you have passed away, Mahmoud; but tell me, just how is the death of the body? I still don't love all of my own body; but now that you have lost yours, do you miss it? That's presumptuous of me, maybe you do have access to your full body, loving, sensual, heavenly and kind and you just don't want to tell us—if so, we'd all want to die, then, eh?

There isn't, to me, a way that poetry enters me and ends there, just remaining inside of me. It reverberates; they bounce around—the words, images, scents of what I write, of what others write, the jumble of it all. The structure of one poem, like a strand of futuristic DNA, can actually compel some of my cells to grow in new ways. My brain cells, my liver cells, my job cells, my social life cells…have all responded to a poem, at one time or another. Poetic phrases, singular sentences, have fed muscles in my diaphragm, the fascia in my torso, replenished the arteries in my shoulders and led me to march against nuclear arms.

My Palestinian friends unknowingly opened me to the poetry in their journey. The food they share, the family life I partic-

ipate in, the horrors and revulsion I am given when I mention their nationality to my old family and friends, are living poems. I believe that poetry doesn't change anything, poetry touches everything, allows everything to be touched. Poetry allows the violent memories of war, which have been handed down to my eyes, to touch the violence my good friends are changing by studying peace here in the U.S. Poems tether longing to connection, intimacy to intimacy, they dovetail desire with satisfaction. One of the fundaments of creation is that everything wants to be touched. In it's simplicity, variety, complex patience, poetry touches everything, and poets are created to be capillaries.

I don't agree, Mahmoud, that "poetry only changes the poet." I believe that poetry is the beat of the deep heart as well as the living chambers of a heart that hears her own beat, and knows her rhythm joins the world.

In Peace,

Amy R. Tighe

Truth

Dorothy Shubow Nelson

University of Massachusetts Boston

dorothy.nelson@umb.edu

There are things that are truths and then there is the indefinable TRUTH of the connection and power that exists between human beings. The first and last stanzas are chants calling for an end to this separation which was created and is maintained brutally and illegally by the colonizers. As a Jewish American woman, the poet Dorothy Shubow Nelson feels no separation between the Arab people and herself, between Palestinians and herself. We cannot control the forces of nature such as rain or drought, although we can severely damage those natural forces. We can control our relationships to each other. She recognizes the great losses brought about by the occupation and projects a deep longing for no separation.

you are my half sister
we have the same father
                    we have been
separated too long

I can stay in the city no more

steel buildings hide your eyes from me
the sand in your hair your wrinkled face

machines and airplanes smother your cries and
the cries of little birds

where are your children
I want to see them (was it a hard birth)

Dorothy Shubow Nelson's book of poems, *The Dream of the Sea,* was published in 2008. Her poems have been published in *Sojourner, The Café Review, Rhythm Magazine, atelier, North Shore North, The Cambridge Tab, Spare Change, The Bridge, The Somerville News, Consequence Magazine,* the Website of the Palace of the Governors in Santa Fe, and the publications of The Boston Conservatory, *The Marquee* and *Illusions.* She has read her work in Cambridge, Boston and New York and on Public Radio. She has presented numerous papers on the teaching of writing and literature at educational conferences including the National Council of Teachers of English, The Conference of College Composition and Communication, The American Literature Association and the Association for the Study of Literature and the Environment. She is a Senior Lecturer in English at UMass Boston. She has also taught at The Boston Conservatory and The University of New Mexico, Albuquerque.

let me see your roses blooming
near the well, the almond trees
the family's garden, the graves

partitions and walls stand between us —
occupation keeps us estranged
did you see the half moon recently low in the sky
I ran to the highway to find the moon

do you have enough water
can I reach you with this page

will this offering call forth water from the dry spring
call forth absent voices whose lips
will kiss stones under stones

here the rain keeps coming, pushing against
the cracks in the frame of this wooden house
there is nothing we can do about this rain

you are my half sister
we have the same father
                                    we have been
separated too long

Darwish Sits In

Robert Lipton

Poet and Writer

roblipton@gmail.com

The poem "Darwish sits in," by poet Robert Lipton, weaves the everyday moments and the larger historical predicament of Palestinians as conveyed through the poetic sense of their late national poet, Mahmoud Darwish. Lipton asks in the poem, What would it take to resurrect Darwish's face, to have it raise its self-flagellation like a theater curtain? The answer is first placed within the well-trod terrain of the poorly diagnosed, the unfortunately lavish. Lipton then explores home incarceration which has the added benefit of accounting for all the Hansels and Gretels, the trail of crumbs, dense black smoke, without a roof and supporting walls, a village covered in wild mustard. These are unsatisfactory results. We are left with the disease of music, a man on a stool, a hissing tea kettle, the final exsanguination of words.

Darwish riffed off the simmering exchange between
his mother-in-law and the border
police recruits, a high little 2 bar interlude

you could hear the dry crackle of olive tree
leaves or it simply could be the feedback

in the monitors

he was told once that the visions
of Christ in the desert were just the wind
charitably blowing from the Mediterranean

down into the Jordan valley, he would strike
the guitar with his palm, like a Dumbek
then thump! the water tower would be shot

off the house.

Robert Lipton has a book of poetry *A Complex Bravery* from Marick Press (2006). His poems have appeared in *New Orleans Quarterly,* and the *Texas Observer,* amongst others. He writes journalistically for the blog Muzzle-watch.org and has published the essay "Bearing witness in the promised land" in "Live from Palestine." He works doing public health/medical research at Beth Israel Deaconess Medical Center in Boston and writes on the philosophy of science/causation.

he was querulous when it came to claw hammer
guitar and the amount of sugar in his Turkish
coffee, sometimes when the moon had darkened

and there was no time to worry about bombing runs
(something like a reminder to practice more)
the dust and the wife telling him to stop watching

water beading and running down the wall next to
the stove, his powers of contemplation were often acute
and badly targeted. He had a little spell of prison

in his picking hand, a nose like Dylan that deflected
children jeering his terrible football skills.

Most of his rattle and hiss was just the Fender
double reverb talking to itself, Darwish likes
a slow rhythm low panicking his left hand driven

arpeggios, counter balanced copter blades lending
a whupping like a Hammond b3. Piedmont
blues? Well, he had issues like the broken bell

of ancestral tone deafness, an analgesic of a voice
he would smoke in that bitter way men of drama
offer, thumb and index finger, pain at inhale

or there would be the burnt tire blues
constantly dickered with, "baby too much trouble
for a smile/I'll love you for your soft umber hills/

anyways, I'll stay a while/"

just a raspy croak, Calandria and rebar, the water
park one block off the Muqatta, adenoidal squeals
of children and the chevron scat of heavy

tracked vehicles marking up the streets, he sits
in an armless chair and listens to cacophony
with no commercial breaks. He will overlook a city

overlooking a city that has no music but the settling

of old stones

American Idols

Joyce Peseroff

University of Massachusetts Boston

joyce.peseroff@umb.edu

*(The Antikythera Mechanism, discovered more than
100 years ago in a Roman shipwreck, was used by an-
cient Greeks to display astronomical cycles. Its system
of gears and cogs never appeared in a machine or
weapon.)*

For ancient Greeks
gears creaked

not in machines but toys.
They cared

who danced hardest,
who played best,

who told the old
story with a twist—

gods lofty
on a pulley.

Beautiful youth
still engage

agora and stage
as their white teeth

approach, retreat,
in tabloids racked

by Lex High juniors
for minimum wage.

Javelins they hurl
on practice fields

beside the Town Pool
wobble and prick

fresh turf. Those old
Greeks didn't

labor-save: slaves
in harness hauled

Achilles' entourage
to war without a cog.

Joyce Peseroff is distinguished lecturer of English and director of the MFA Program at UMass Boston. Her four books of poems are *The Hardness Scale, A Dog in the Lifeboat, Mortal Education,* and *Eastern Mountain Time.* She has been managing editor and associate poetry editor of *Ploughshares,* and edited *The Ploughshares Poetry Reader, Robert Bly: When Sleepers Awake,* and *Simply Lasting: Writers on Jane Kenyon.* Her poems and reviews appear in the *Atlantic Monthly, Southern Review, New York Times Book Review, The Women's Review of Books,* and the online journal *Slate.*

Wreck

Fady Joudah

Palestinian-American Poet, Physician, and Translator

isdoud@yahoo.com

Over treasure and land some texts will say it had
Little to do with slavery or the newly

Discovered yellow planet
Few men watched the glaciers recede

From shuttles they had built
During the hemorrhage years

When they had gathered the genes
Down from the ledges:

I'll be a fig or a sycamore tree
Or without hands

By then doctors and poets
Would have found a cure for prayer

•••

Fady Joudah, a Palestinian-American poet and physician, was the 2007 winner of the Yale Series of Younger Poets Competition for his collection of poems *The Earth in the Attic*, which was published by Yale University Press in April 2008. Joudah was born in Austin, Texas, in 1971 to Palestinian refugee parents, and grew up in Libya and Saudi Arabia. He returned to the United States to study to become a doctor, first attending the University of Georgia in Athens, and then the Medical College of Georgia, before completing his medical training at the University of Texas. Joudah currently practices as an ER physician in Houston, Texas. He has also volunteered abroad with the humanitarian organization Doctors Without Borders. Joudah's poetry has been published in a variety of publications, including *Poetry* magazine, *Iowa Review, Kenyon Review, Drunken Boat, Prairie Schooner* and *Crab Orchard*. In 2006, he published *The Butterfly's Burden*, a collection of recent poems by Palestinian poet Mahmoud Darwish translated from Arabic. He was a finalist for the 2008 PEN Award for Poetry in Translation for his translation of Mahmoud Darwish's *The Butterfly's Burden* (Copper Canyon Press, 2007). The translation won the Saif Ghobash-Banipal Prize for Arabic Literary translation from the Society of Authors in the United Kingdom.

Or have you shoved the door shut
In the face of the dark?

Have your body and light the trap
Of retribution doing unto you

What it does to others? You protest
In the streets and newspapers

And I leave for a faraway land
Where with pill and scalpel

And a distant reckoning
If he should lick his lips

Or clench his fist I shall
Find his second left toe

Infected puffy from a bump
Lance it

Squeeze out the pus and offer

Him an antibiotic I can't refuse
Therefore I am

• • •

The first time I saw you it was hot I was fed up
The second time your wife gave birth to a macerated boy

I had nothing to tell you
About letting go of the dying

In the morning you were gone
Had carried your father back to your house
His cracked skull

I didn't know that was your wife
When I raised my voice

To those who were praying
From behind the wall to keep it down

I was trying to listen to your baby's heartbeat
With a gadget a century old

• • •

Anemic
From so much loss giving birth

If you give blood in the desert you won't
Get it back not your iron pills or magic hat

I put your thin
Hemoglobin up to the light and called out

To the donors Donors
If you want to know your blood type

And it's a match
You must donate

Few came some indifferent to my condition
Having not heard of it
And willing anyhow

• • •

And the world is south
The night a bandit with gasoline

And I'm your dancing lizard mirth
I put my one arm up

And bring my one foot down on a hot zinc top
The nearest hospital was the dawn:

She didn't know her daughter on her back was
The entry wound and she the exit

She ran a brothel so
The officer said it was

Where the rebels came and went
And ran into the government boys

Her girl's femur the size of the bullet

• • •

A mother offers not necessarily
Sells her one-eyed son

For an education if you'll bring him back
And stone dust for one
With congenital illness

And little boy with malaria
Same old gas

Money mixed with blood
Transfusion the doctor's perfect record

Broken, nobility of taking
A life you

Who must walk to and from your house
The jeep's upkeep
The donkey-cart ambulance

• • •

The mind in the field
The brine in the field

Whether I
Is a diphthong codependent on

What isn't there to stay in the field

The good you act is equal
To the good you doubt

Most have lost many

You are either prosperous
Or veteran in the field

• • •

One boot left behind

One-boot-photo I wanted
For a book cover the boot

Military black the quad a clinic's

Special forces spun
By his dangling heels from

The pick-up truck rushed
To a central town altered combative

With two scalp lacerations and blood
In his auditory canal:

I was a lover of loss, I tossed
The boot in the capital of suffering

The Lost and Found Warehouse

Shaari Neretin

Social Worker and Activist

———————————————————

shneretin@gmail.com

Abstract: This is a brief fictional exploration of what happens over time to lost, stolen, forgotten, forfeited, and mis/displaced experiences, both internal (affective) and external (actual events). In this tale, I imagine a place—"The Lost and Found Warehouse"—where experiences are stored in relative security but almost certain obscurity. A.G. Green, Middle Manager, oversees the Warehouse and makes efforts to keep its contents organized and available to the general public in order that they might someday retrieve that which they have lost. I did not consciously write this story with Mahmoud Darwish or the Palestinian Diaspora in mind. A dear friend, a Palestinian sister, read it and because it resonated for her, she asked that I submit it for review for this special 2009 issue of *Human Architecture* on Mahmoud Darwish. As it turns out, this serendipitous occurrence is in keeping with Darwish's philosophy on writing and reading. In an interview in *BOMB Magazine*, Darwish stated, "My happiest times are when the public reads and interprets an aspect of my poem that was not clear to me. The life of the poet is conditioned by the reader." (2002, issue 81, www.bombsite.com/issues/81/articles/2520) Indeed. May your reading continue to condition the lives of the poet within us all.

———————————————————

PRELIMINARY REFLECTIONS: A WITNESS, A TELLER, AND A KEEPER

"There is enough of unconsciousness to liberate things from their history. And there is enough of history to liberate unconsciousness from its ascension."[1]

Mahmoud Darwish is a "teller," a wordsmith, a poet, and a meaning maker. He has become one of the strongest voices that speak of the Palestinian condition. And yet Darwish, like many artists and poets, is not just a *voice* for a Palestinian consciousness. Through his life, his work and his person, he has become a repository for the many feel-

———————————————————

Shaari Neretin has a Masters in Social Work and is a Licensed Independent Clinical Social Worker. She is an activist for peace and justice between the Israelis and the Palestinians. Her most recent article, "Creating Temporary Shelter in the Psychotherapeutic Space: Reflections of a Psychotherapist Working with Immigrant Women" will be published in summer of 2009 in *Crossing Borders, Making Homes, Stories of Resilient Women* (D. Cathcart, D. Llera & E. Roffman, editors). Ms. Neretin is also a visual artist, a painter who mostly paints portraits of portraits. She is an M.Path, an unofficial designation for an informal group of friends and acquaintances who happen to be highly sensitive individuals.

———————————————————

[1] Darwish M. (2007) "In Her Absence I Created her Image" in *The Butterfly's Burden*, Washington/Copper Canyon Press.

ings and thoughts, hopes and desires of the Palestinian Diaspora—the dispossessed, the oppressed, the lost and the invisible. He is the rage, he is the justice, he is the keeper and he is the teller. He remembers, he experiences and he tells.

I am not a teller. I am a witness. I am a psychotherapist. I have worked with those in exile, and I have worked with those who live in their home city, state and country of origin and feel displaced. I have sat with people who dig deep into their physical and psychological journeys to figure out what they need now to cope with the experience of being displaced, abandoned and restless. I have been witness to and suffered myself due to countless losses of consciousness due to small and large infractions of the human spirit, of injustice. I have often felt out of place but I remain in my "homeland."

It is hard to bring forth and make meaning of all that assaults us, especially when we are forced out of place.

But I am a witness, perhaps a keeper, but not a teller.

Darwish, like the middle manager A.G. Green, who is the protagonist in the short story I offer below, is aware that he has limited power to change reality [1] but he does have access to a broad range of emotional and psychic states and seems to believe in its power and authority.[2] Darwish and A.G. Green are both keepers, protectors and guardians of powerful experiences, not all their own, and both must do the best that they can in their work to honor and care for these experiences.

Indeed the complicated internal and external circumstances that makes up the Palestinian identity and it's physical land, necessitates a keen and humble eye and mind to contain, categorize, make sense of and keep alive the multitude of experiences and expressions that are lost to others as they struggle to maintain their memory, or their parents' memories, and/or their desire for their homeland.

I did not write this story with Mahmoud Darwish nor the Palestinian Diaspora in mind. A dear friend, a Palestinian sister, read this story and it resonated for her. She asked that I submit it for the special 2009 issue of *Human Architecture* on Mahmoud Darwish. I am pleased to have been able to do this for it is in keeping with Darwish's philosophy on telling. He states, "My happiest times are when the public reads and interprets an aspect of my poem that was not clear to me. The life of the poet is conditioned by the reader."[3]

Now, perhaps, for this brief moment, I become the witness, the keeper and the teller.

THE LOST AND FOUND WAREHOUSE

"First we take years to think and analyze—sometimes forfeiting full lives to our relative material inactivity—and then for many reasons, some quite unreasonable if

---

[1] In the aforementioned interview in *BOMB Magazine*, Darwish states, "Then, I became close to the Israeli Communist Party. This introduced me to the notion that poetry can be an instrument of change. I took this very seriously until I arrived at my own conclusion that poetry changes nothing. It may have an effect on how people feel, but it has not effect on reality. The only person it changes is the poet himself." (www.bombsite.com/issues/81/articles/2520)

[2] Ibid (www.bombsite.com/issues/81/articles/2520), Darwish speaks of his youth and his burgeoning interest in becoming a poet, "I began to dream of becoming a poet. I believed the poet was a mysterious figure with superhuman faculties."

[3] IBID, FALL 2002, NYC/NY.

you ask me, we don't show up for the big hurrah." —A.G. Green, Managing Supervisor

What had once been a lost and found box became, by necessity, a warehouse, a huge, open space that was absolutely indispensable to house all the lost feelings, thoughts, and desires of so many who had never come to reclaim them.

No more withered by aged cardboard liquor boxes ("after all"—they thought— "why replace such a container when it was so rarely used?") that are half sagging and stained, wetted by seasonal losses. No more discarded crates that sit not quite in a corner but near enough to one so as to direct the very occasional seeker to the lost and found box that is "in the corner." It was a valuable service indeed to the individual but unlimited-ness preempted this humble humanitarian gesture.

No, things got too big for this box. With so many opportunities—by chance or by intention—to leave behind just a small bit of themselves and not notice for years, if ever, that in fact they had lost something, the quantity became overwhelming. And the fact is that even if someone did, at some point, realize that they were missing something, the process of recuperation is a painstaking undertaking, often involving years and years of a particular kind of singular focus. So as you can see, storage space became absolutely indispensable.

The fact remains that to find that which was lost is a backbreaking task. First one has to retrace their steps, thoughtfully, carefully and one must be able to do so and keep track of their steps while enduring the countless interruptions that constitute the mundane chores of everyday life. This act of finding is both a physical and mental feat. One needs to go backwards—heels first, toes next (this being in and of itself a very unsettling order of events for how can we feel grounded if we are walking backwards?)— trying to remember a series of moments, hours, days, weeks, months, years—so that one may invent a threadlike connection to the actual place that they probably had that loss. It has been known to necessitate years and years of backwards walking all the while standing erect and looking forward while in the present. Just thinking about this makes me dizzy. And I assure you that this is by no means a linear process. Nope, sometimes these threads of remembering are erroneous and one needs to begin the process again.

And then, to terrible effect, when there is success in identifying where the loss occurred, often those places either no longer exist or they have express shipped their items to the Warehouse long ago. (As I told you earlier, no more "corner" boxes. They all end up here one way or another and in a quite timely fashion I might add. Our system, while not exactly comprised of high-end technology, does work quite well on that end of things.) You can only imagine how this can drain the hope out of anyone.

Mind you, not everyone performs the laborious acts of detective work to find what they have lost. Some folks don't even necessarily know that they have lost anything at all. There might be a sense that something has gone missing, but the preference is to either ignore this or to imagine that one is just imagining what they are feeling. Well, at least that's my theory on why so many find their way here. You know that feeling though, don't you?—we all do. You're at the front door in the morning, checking and re-checking your pockets, making sure you have keys, money, drivers license, etc. And yet, still you are not quite sure that you have everything.

No, the Warehouse is full of lost feelings, thoughts and desires and there is a high probability that many of these items will not be moved, reclaimed nor repossessed. And yet the Warehouse still stands, receiving the shipments, filling up the space and in the end functioning as if it was functional. It's a one-way street, I tell you, the items come in and rarely leave. If I had my way, things would change so that the system could work better, but then…well, I'll get to this in just a bit.

Let me tell you a little about the physical plant of The Lost and Found Warehouse. It is quite a large storage area, your typical industrial steel warehouse with five, no make it six, levels counting the basement. From the outside, it's a kind of pitiful sight, but on the inside it's not so bad. It has surprisingly good natural light. We have a southern exposure, so this is, as you might imagine, quite useful when we are trying to help the occasional customer to locate something. It is also a very nice benefit for the employees, and myself—it really makes the day better to have some sunshine in our midst.

Unfortunately like many large industrial storage sites—places where products of the quick producing, fast paced, blah, blah, blah modern world are stored (we've all heard and critiqued the pitfalls of industrialization and modernism, but as the saying goes, there is no way to fight it because you can't turn back the hands of time) it's not so easy to get here. If you don't have a car, or a friend with a car, or taxi money, unfortunately you are plain out of luck. It is not accessible by train or any form of mass transportation, which is a shame because truly, perhaps more people might decide that they could set out on a journey to find what they had lost—they could take all those steps backwards and even make that final connection—"Aha, that is where it probably is" and set out to actually reclaim that which was lost.

But then again, it could not reasonably be so that it is the lack of transportation that inhibits a trip to the Lost and Found Warehouse. There are so many deterrents, really, if you think about it. People have a lot of work to do, or they are sick or have a toothache, or "dinner is getting cold."

I got my job here quite by accident, or actually, maybe it was by intention but certainly not my own. You know how they say that some people are born leaders, or born losers, or born to _____—well you can fill in the blank. Well, it seems that I was born to be living my life situated within the realm of lost feelings, thoughts and desires. I suppose if that was what I was born to do then my vocation in this lifetime has been to figure out how to catalog, contain and ultimately return them to those to whom they have been lost.

Unfortunately, I didn't get the right kind of training, nor education, or at least not the exact kind I would need to step up the ladder of success, so here I am in the middle world of middle managers who know too much and are not blessed with authority to make decisions and take action on their own.

You may wonder then, who exactly are my bosses, and to be perfectly frank with you, I ask myself this question more frequently than I would care to admit to you. I mean not only is it difficult not to be able to tell someone exactly who you work for, but honestly there are many times I wish I had a stronger sense of my bosses for any number of reasons. Sometimes you just want authority to come down and structure the chaos. Make some big decisions. Make decisions for you. I mean, even if they couldn't figure out how to do this with the content of the Warehouse which I completely understand (as we all know how complicated it is to deal with these things)—the least they could do is make some brilliant and future thinking decisions that would make it easier for me and my employees to sort these things out.

What I have thus far surmised in my time here is that I don't really have a boss. There is a vague but very large Board of Directors that oversees the Warehouse and makes sure that it keeps going, but they aren't exactly visionaries. I mean, I could really use some help in both slowing down the pace of what comes in here or at least one day a week when the doors are closed, but they allow shipments to come in, small or large, at any time of day and any day of the week.

So, I am charged with the task of keeping it all together here, in spite of the fact that we all know that lost feelings, thoughts and desires can get way out of control and desperately need a great deal of structure and organization.

Being a middle manager in the Lost and Found Warehouse is no easy task, no siree, not at all. I have to keep organizing and re-organizing because it always seems that there is more coming in than going out. I don't really have fellow workers because being middle management, I am charged with telling others what to do, even if it is just small things like "arrange that aisle so that nobody trips and there is no lawsuit." And like I said, because I don't really have authority I can't really change anything, like when workers get breaks, or time off, or cost of living allowances. Nope, I just get to tell them what to do, small tasks, and of course, because I appear not to be a visionary because my bosses are not visionaries, then I am not particularly respected around here. Middle management is a lonely place indeed.

The workers don't really know what I do for them and I suppose even if they did know they wouldn't necessarily appreciate me more for it. And the Board of Directors don't really know what I do for this Warehouse to keep it going and to keep the workers happy, and with them too, even if they did know it, I doubt they would be very appreciative, because they are paying attention to the Warehouse just enough to keep it going. It's not exactly a heartfelt investment of their time. Although I did hear that at one point, many of them were so very eager to join the Board and they believed in the Warehouse and imagined that it would facilitate a sense of community. It does seem like such a simple and humble gesture to store lost items and hope they are returned. But I guess the Board got disillusioned at some point and turned their philanthropic gestures elsewhere.

I really do do things that make the workers' lives better—really—and it is important to me that at least you believe this. Perhaps you want an outline or a strategy plan, but I don't have one because even if I did no one but me would pay attention. But I'll give you a brief overview of my job responsibilities and how it helps my workers and the Warehouse and even how it benefits the Board of Directors.

One of the most important functions of my job is to carefully evaluate each item that comes into the Warehouse and make sure that it can be contained until someone comes and claims it. You'd be really surprised how out of control these lost feelings, thoughts and desires can be. Things can get really crazy here and that means the workers as well. So it is my job to make sure these feelings don't get under the skins of the workers so that they can keep doing their job effectively, even if this means that often I am stung, bitten, smitten, hurt, dirtied, cut, offended and many other things by all these lost feelings, thoughts and desires that I need to log in.

The workers don't quite understand how much I shield them and that's a shame really. It would be nice to have some appreciation of just how much I take on for them.

Mind you, on an everyday basis, I don't feel like a victim or a martyr. It is true that sometimes I think that my work makes me suffer too much at the end of the day (though there really isn't an end to the day—its more like when I doze off for a few hours—for as you know middle managers get little sleep because we are always so worried about what we are supposed to do according to our superiors but so constrained in what we really can do) or I feel so lonely in my position as middle manager, but for the most part, I am oblivious to the intensity and the enormity of the task at hand, that is until I sit down and think about it.

So, I do get "emotional" depending on how the day is going but because I am a middle-aged man and a middle manager, expressing any feeling is out of the question. And I do mean out of the question. Even my job description mentions something about "no affect stimulation at any time." The words explain that the uncontained expression of any feelings is bound to excite the employees that would then cause a diminishment of focus on the job they have to do. Unfortunately, while I understand this need to keep order at the Warehouse, which often does mean not getting involved in confusing and confused states of mind and heart, they don't offer any alternatives, such as extra breaks after a particularly trying off load of a truck, or a day long retreat so that we can clear the air and get on with our work.

So on some days, I spend just a few minutes extra in the very dimly lit restroom. I carefully remove my worn grey fedora and rest it on the edge of the sink. Then I look into the mirror, adjust my posture and begin to stare at myself and make sure I am really me and really there and I wait to see what happens. Sometimes, a few tears will start to form in both eyes, but never in the same place or at the same time. I watch as these vague forms begin to slowly make the trip down my cheeks. I contemplate the pace and form of these tears and feel just a bit grateful that I have them, that they are not lost.

But that's not what is most important to tell you about regarding my job and this Warehouse.

While one might think that I am rewarded most for my performance regarding customer satisfaction, truly, the Cataloging and Containment of that which enters through these doors is what I am most valued for and is the most formidable part of my job given that not many customers show up here. So, our job tasks focus mainly on the receipt and storage of items.

Here they are below. I am reproducing these papers so that you can get an idea of what the work is like here, both in the tasks and the evaluation of job performance. But please, don't pass this around because if my "bosses" see them, it could mean it would mean the loss of my job.

(I am so excited to be able to review these with you. I so rarely get an opportunity like this.)

1. Cataloguing Protocol for the Lost and Found Warehouse Receivable Items

Cataloging Protocol for The Lost and Found Warehouse Receivable Items

1. Cataloging of items received in the Warehouse must be formally entered into the Log.
2. All categories in the Log must be properly filled out. These categories are as follows: Date Received, Date Shipped, Shipping location (where the item was shipped from), Proper Categorization of content of shipment (see Containment Protocol for the Lost and Found Warehouse of Receivable items for further instruction on categorization), and full name of the Person Receiving Shipment.
3. Once the Cataloging Log is properly filled out, then The Containment Protocol must be followed.

2. Containment Protocol for the Lost and Found Warehouse of Receivable Items

Containment Protocol for the Lost and Found Warehouse of Receivable Items

1. Given the highly unpredictable nature of items received in the Warehouse, caution is of the greatest importance in dealing with these items.
2. Given the highly unpredictable nature of items received in the Warehouse, a cursory evaluation will serve as the basis for Categorization. If during this cursory evaluation, the item seems to be of high risk, immediately call your supervisor who will follow the High Risk Containment Protocol
3. After completion of the cursory evaluation, check the box in the Catalog Log whether the item falls under Feelings, Desires or Thoughts.
4. While it might be difficult to be absolutely sure of the category, it is nonetheless completely necessary to check only one box in the Log.
5. Place the item in a color-coded folder and store in a box with same folders. Be sure that the box is dated.

3. High Risk Containment Protocol

High Risk Containment Protocol

Please be aware that this protocol is confidential and should only be the knowledge of supervisors! Any deviation from this will be cause for immediate dismissal!

1. Remove all personnel from the immediate area.
2. Place item in plastic container and immediately put the lid on it.
3. Put color-coded label on the container, identifying the contents as close to one of the three categories as possible.
4. Carefully store item in containment area.
5. Log the information in the High Risk Containment Protocol Log.

On that rare occasion, when a customer actually comes into the Warehouse looking for something, often they are not quite sure what it is that they are looking for. It is my job to keep teaching and coaching my employees to be able to gently guide the customer towards what they might be needing to find without too much pushing of our own agenda (i.e. if one aisle is overflowing for example, the customer service representative might be inclined to steer the customer towards that aisle so that we can get rid of what seems like overstock). It's so easy to just go where it is obvious.

I have a tip list or a cheat sheet that I have been in the process of writing for some time. This is what I hope will be my lasting contribution to the success of the Warehouse. My legacy, if you will. This list will be specifically geared to help insure customer satisfaction and protect my workers. I don't seem to be able though to ever get it to the point where I can hand it out to the Warehouse employees, because always there are things that seem not right.

For example, no matter how many times I revise it, this list always begins with the same suggestion: "proceed with caution but with care and grace."

Now the reason I keep revising this list is because the employees can't seem to get through that first tip. They stutter on the word and then smirk when they get to the grace part. I am never really sure if the reason for their smirk is a defense against having stuttered or if they just truly don't know how to react when they think about care and grace. Embarrassment maybe?

Professional Tips for Good Customer Service and Satisfaction

Compiled and Written by _____, after years of professional service as Middle Manager in the Lost and Found Warehouse

1. Proceed with Caution but with Care and Grace
2. The Customer is not always right, but always treat them as if they were. Often, they don't know yet that they are not right, but they will eventually get there and need your assistance in numerous ways.
3. Good hygiene and clean, sharp clothing make a person attractive and approachable.
4. Be timely and considerate in your treatment of your fellow workers.
5. Always check and re-check your paperwork so that when assisting a customer, you know exactly what the Warehouse contents are.
6. Be sympathetic but not overly so when a customer comes in and is confused and afraid. Don't distract them from their search by focusing on their confusion.
7. Be confident with the customer and the customer will be confident with you and with themselves.
8. Finally, know that you can count on me to help you in any way in improving on your job performance.

Sincerely yours,

A.G. Green, Managing Supervisor

Mantra for Mahmoud Darwish

Jack Hirschman

Poet

aggiefalk@hotmail.com

Poet Jack Hirschman composed the poem "Mantra for Mahmoud Darwish" in the French language (only the second poem he has ever written in French) in the home of his French translator, the poet Gilles B. Vachon, for an event celebrating the life and work of Darwish which was held early in December 2008 at a Grenoble restaurant. The form of the mantra is a form he has used once before when, many years ago, he mantrad the name of Jalaluddin Rumi in the same manner. The form is intended to evoke, through repetition, and iconized the image of the poet. In the instance, especially the phrase "the new Palestine," Hirschman wanted to project forward into the future the significance of this great Palestinian poet's work. Shortly after Darwish's death, five poets enthusiastic about his poetry—Nina Serrano, the Palestinian-American poet Deema Shehabi, Neeli Cherkovski, Leonore Weiss and Hirschman himself—read Darwish's poetry over Pacifica's KPFA Radio in Berkeley, CA, just as comrades in Grenoble sounded Darwish's work in that Grenoble restaurant. An English translation of Hirschman's poem "Mantra for Mahmoud Darwish" appearing herein (next page) was prepared by UMass Boston honors alumni and special issue co-editor Erica Mena.

Mah
Mahmoud
Mahmouddar
Mahmouddarwish
Mahmouddarwishgrande
Mahmouddarwishgrandepo
Mahmouddarwishgrandepoet
Mahmouddarwishgrandepoetla
Mahmouddarwishgrandepoetlanou
Mahmouddarwishgrandepoetlanouveau
Palestine chantera tes mots comme des cris
Incendiaires et pleins de compassion dans les oreilles
      Du lendemain glorieux

Jack Hirschman has published more than 100 books of poetry, half of them translations from 9 languages. He is former poet laureate of the city of San Francisco and, as the poet-in-residence with the friends of the San Francisco public library he organized the highly successful San Francisco International Poetry Festival that brought poets from nineteen countries to read in July 2009.

MANTRA FOR MAHMOUD DARWISH

Mah
Mahmoud
Mahmouddar
Mahmouddarwish
Mahmouddarwishgreat
Mahmouddarwishgreatpo
Mahmouddarwishgreatpoet
Mahmouddarwishgreatpoetthe
Mahmouddarwishgreatpoetthenew
Mahmouddarwishgreatestpoetthenew
Palestine will sing your words like cries
Incendiary and full of compassion sung for the ears
        Of a glorious tomorrow

(by Jack Hirschman, translated by Erica Mena)

Darwish and the Meaning of Palestine

Leila Farsakh

University of Massachusetts Boston

Abstract: Darwish's poetry was a central part of what is to be a Palestinian and to be an Arab. By weaving the personal and the political, Darwish gave a voice to the Palestinian struggle for self determination, as much as to the human inner quest for love and survival. I grew up learning his poems, hearing them sung by famous Arab singers, repeated in worldwide demonstrations of solidarity with the Palestinian people. His departure left me, and a whole generation of Arabs, deeply bereaved for his death represented not simply the loss of a great poet, but also the necessity to re-question the meaning of Palestine. Darwish's poetry reminds us that Palestine is exile as much as home, a struggle for political justice as much as for what it is to be a cosmopolitan citizen. It remains the quintessential human struggle for dignity, justice and humanity, globally as much as locally.

It was a year ago that I was in Palestine attending a poetry recital of Mahmoud Darwish. It was the first that I ever heard him recite his poetry live. I did not know that it was the last, for him as well as for me, as he died 3 weeks afterwards, in Texas, 6000 miles away from Ramallah. The concert/recital was in July, in the beautifully constructed cultural palace of the hilly Palestinian city-dubbed future capital, built with the money of the international donor community to prove its commitment to the Palestinian cause. It was a contribution to enable Palestinian art to flourish in the midst of the confines of over 145 Israeli checkpoints, in the Bantustans that they were actually living in.

Darwish was austere and the audience ecstatic. He stood on the stage with a certain shyness and started to recite his poetry as a lover flirting with his beloved, a lover that has aged and was wondering what was the meaning of it all, all this life of his, all this struggle of his, all this trajectory that he and his country have gone through and which his poetry so intimately weaved together. "I am from there" he recalled, and "the earth is closing onto us" he reminded us just as "there is fog over the bridge" the bridge of exile as much as of return, only to ask in the end to just "let me down here," for while I am tired of the journey. He said more and more, recited old and new poems, and read them with such a sensual voice that made you desire as much as cry, want to hold him, touch him, delay the recital's ending only to accept that you cannot; his poetry is too deep a part of you and of Palestine to be contained in a word, symbol or act.

The death of Darwish came as shock to

Professor Farsakh holds a Ph.D. from the University of London (2003), and an MPhil from the University of Cambridge in the UK (1990). She has published on questions related to Palestinian labor migration, the Oslo Peace Process, and international migration in a wide range of journals including *Middle East Journal*, *European Journal of Development Research*, *Journal of Palestine Studies* and *Le Monde Diplomatique*. Her book, *Palestinian Labor Migration to Israel: Labor, Land and Occupation*, was published by Routledge Press in Fall 2005.

me and, I would add, to all my generation of Palestinians and Arabs, all those who grew up learning his poems, hearing them sung by famous Arab singers, such as Marcel Khaleefeh, repeated in demonstrations of solidarity with the Palestinian people. I felt bereaved, deeply bereaved, for his death represented not simply the loss of a great poet, but also the closing of a very important chapter of the life of Palestine. It forced on me, and I suppose many other Palestinians, to re-question the meaning of Palestine, which Darwish has often done and struggled with. Darwish's poetry was as a central part of who I am, of what it is to be a Palestinian, of what it is to struggle for your humanity globally as much as locally, of what it is to become a cosmopolitan cause, a cosmopolitan citizen.

I was born in 1967, few months after the 1967 war, the Naska, or debacle as it is called in Arabic. I was born in exile and my family became de facto refugees. Darwish was just 25 years old, he had started already to write poetry, had already lived the Nakba, the catastrophe, when his native village Al-Birwa was wiped out with Israel's creation, and was already in prison in 1962 for opposing Israel's military rule over the Palestinians. He had already written his poem, "I long for the bread of my mother, the coffee of my mother and the touch of my mother … and I desire my life because if I die I would be ashamed of the tears of my mother." This is the first poem I learned in school when I was six year old, it is the one we sang on mother's day ever since. For a little girl just trying to come to term with her separation from her mother, it made perfect sense. For all Palestinians trying to come to term with the loss of Palestine, with exile, it could not be more poignant.

I grew up in exile in many Arab countries. In all of these places, Darwish accompanied me in my Arabic classes as he did my relatives and friends going to school in Jordan, Lebanon, Kuwait, Yemen and Dubai, among other places. "Write down I am an Arab, and my ID card number is … I have 8

children and the 9th is about to come," wrote Darwish in a poem that came to represent Palestinian assertion of their Arab identity, of their right to self determination. Growing up in the US or France, it resonates with every Arab ostracized and oppressed by a colonial power. For Mona, my friend growing up in Nazareth in schools that censored what Israel considered Darwish's "inflammatory poetry," her teacher used to sneak the poems and get the students to learn it. Mona, who would became a teacher herself, would not stop reciting Darwish to her kids and friends. That was before Darwish became legal, when Israel's Minister of Culture Yossi Beilin allowed his poems to be included in the Israeli curricula after the Peace process in 1993, only to see these removed after the Sharon government in 2001.

Darwish gave a voice to the Palestinians trying to affirm their existence in a world that negated them and their rights. He did it by always weaving the personal with the political, with a lyric that echoed the magic of classical Arab poetry albeit by completely transforming its traditional structure. He left Haifa in 1969 to go to study in Moscow only to move to Cairo, the heart of Arab culture at the time, to then join the "Revolution" in Beirut in 1972. He became a member of Palestinian Liberation Organization, expressed its quest for freedom and self-determination, composed its anti-colonial third-worldist struggle in his famous *Nuptial* ('Aras) volume. Darwish also wrote Arafat's speech at the United Nations' General Assembly in November 1974, where he presented to the world the Palestinian cause, affirming their right of Return to their land. "I appeal to you to enable our people to establish national independent sovereignty over its own land ….I have come bearing an olive branch and a freedom fighter's gun. Do not let the olive branch fall from my hand."

But the world took away the olive tree and the gun, and watched, rather than defended, the Palestinians as they were denied their most basic rights to life. In 1982, Israel invaded south Lebanon in a campaign intending to wipe out the PLO. The Palestinians came under heavy Israeli artillery and airplane attacks, were besieged under the barrels of death and fear, trapped in heat of the Beirut summer for over 88 days, living yet more fear and death. Darwish wrote his *Memory for Forgetfulness* then, a memory whose forgetfulness becomes all the more impossible after the massacres of Sabra and Shatila in September 1982. The Palestinians were again on the route of exile, this time even further away from Palestine, in Tunis, this time further away from the refugee camps in Lebanon, Jordan and Syria, where refugees were left to their demise, to more war and misery in Lebanon, to near-forgetfulness in all the other diasporas.

For me the 1982 war was a turning point in my consciousness as a Palestinian. Darwish helped me articulate my political consciousness as I was turning 15 years of age. He wrote the *Epic of Beirut* and *Siege of the Sea's Praises* in 1984. He is most remembered by my generation with his epic Ahmad Al-Arabia, Ahmad the Arab. I might well not be living in the refugee camps of Beirut or Syria, I still remain Palestinian. I might not be in Nablus or Haifa, but I am still Palestinian. I might not have lived the Nakba or the daily life of the six day war in 1967, the Naksa, I remain Palestinian. I was still living the exile of Dubai, an Arab city that refused to give me citizenship rights. I was deprived of returning to my father's house in Palestine, where my grandmother, aunts and cousins still lived. I was made to feel impotent as I watched the Palestinians being killed and massacred while other states paid lip services without stopping the killing. I did not belong anywhere and yet I was related by blood as much as by consciousness to those dying to return home. Palestine meant exile as much as home, meant a struggle for justice as much as a quest for some peace.

Darwish carried his exile around with him, as much as I and all those living outside Palestine did. After Beirut, he went to Tunis only to decide that Paris is more adequate as a refuge. He oscillated between Paris, Jordan and Tunis, making his poetry acquire a deeper cosmopolitan essence. He carried the Palestinian experience beyond its reality of dispossession and into the universality of human struggle for dignity and survival. He widened its Arab foundation and all the literary Arab texts he draws upon by weaving the Roman and Greek tragedies, the genocide of the Indians, the loss of Andalusia, and the Mongol invasion into his stanzas. By the eruption of the first Intifada in December 1987, the Palestinians were celebrities, tragedies and not simply terrorists. They were "children of stones" defying Israeli tanks in Gaza and West Bank to claim their independence. By the early 1990s they were the last anti-colonial movement still lingering on after the fall of the Berlin Wall.

But Darwish also struggled with wanting to just be human, with how to reconcile the image of the hero/victim with that of a man just eager to live a simple, trivial life. If Palestine was the muse, the mother, the cause and the home, he negotiated with it and his intimacy, his love and his deepest existential struggles. Darwish was always a lover, and his poetry was as important to my identity as a Palestinian as it was to being a woman. His *Bed of the Stranger* tickled my love stories, set free our love demons, echoed my, and other women's, struggle to simply be who I am, "a woman nothing more or less," accepted for what I am not for what I am expected to be, not carrying the weight of patriarchy nor the burden of idealized romanticized fetish. I remain embraced by "the exile of man in woman and of woman in man." In *Why Did you Leave the Horse Alone*, Darwish dwells further on our inner exile, on our loneliness as we seek to live with others, or, better maybe, without them. In *The Mural* he asked again what is mine and what is for the cause, what belongs to me and what is there for the others.

For the cause never leaves him, nor could it, but he was not going to let others define it for him. In 1988, he wrote the PLO's

Palestinian Declaration of Independence, which became the basis of the Palestinian State. He was in Tunis and then in Geneva as Arafat officially recognized Israel and UN resolution 242. He was a witness to the initiation of the peace process in 1993 and, like many Palestinians, was able to return in 1994. My father too returned to his birth place. I, and many of my generation and younger Palestinians, were also able to go and reside in the West Bank and Gaza to build the institutions of the new independent State, to forge our own personal relation with Palestine, meet the larger family, create new friends, discover the undulated olive tree hills, the warmth of the Mediterranean sea and the shine of Jerusalem and other cities.

But it remained always a question as to what and where we were returning. Israel, who refused Darwish's return after he left in 1969, welcomed him in 1994. But he received no Israeli ID and had no sovereign Palestinian passport. He thus could not, in principle, be inside Israeli 1948 borders, in his native village or where he used to live. The Oslo peace process defined the limits of his, and other Palestinians', mobility within the confines of the Palestinians autonomy, a fragmented territory over less than 22% of historic Palestine, within an anatomized West Bank and Gaza segmented by barred wires and eight meter high wall. He opened a house in Ramallah and started again to oscillate between it, Jordan and Paris. Palestine, the struggle for a Palestinian State, seemed not simply to continue to unfold as a tragedy; it was risking of becoming a farce. Israel refused to retreat from the land it occupied, and the Palestinian leadership was unable to alter the deep unequal power structure it entered with it. The International community watched again, refusing to hold Israel accountable to international law while alleviating its sense of guilt by pouring billions of dollars to the Palestinians in an attempt to prevent them from starvation.

Darwish refused to be part of this process of trivialization of the Palestinian cause.

Palestine is not a humanitarian problem, as he and Arafat reminded us in the late 1960s. It is a political struggle. It still remains the issue today because it remains an anti-colonial struggle that has not been resolved. It is the epic of the victim of the eternal victim. It is ever present because it accentuates the unresolved relation between the East and the West, the "us" and "them," the "one" and the "other." Darwish often reminded us of entangled relation with the "other," of the Israeli who oppresses, dispossesses, and kills, but who also loves, as his early poem "Between Rita and Me is a Rifle" already said, who is also trapped with the Palestinian as his "Ready Scenario" explains, who can only reach her humanity by giving up its power.

Darwish died before he saw the latest Israeli war on Gaza. He had already witnessed the disarray of the Palestinian leadership, and the immunity with which Israeli violation of international law has been received by the international community. He despaired but did not give up. As he said in his last recital and postmortem volume, *I Do Not Want for This Poem to End*. As much as he remained attached to life he remained attached to Palestine, but he was aware that it is "for another poet to complete the scenario that is still unfinished." As I grief his loss, submerge myself in his latest volume, I wonder what my generation and the one after me will do. I know though that Palestine remains the quintessential human struggle for dignity, justice and humanity and this is why it remains alive.

As he so beautifully reminds us:
We have on this earth what makes life
worth living:
On this earth, the lady of earth,
Mother of all beginnings
Mother of all ends.
She was called… Palestine.
She came to be called … Palestine.
My Lady, because you are my Lady,
I am worthy of life

Why the Solidarity?: South Asian Activism for Palestine

Rajini Srikanth

University of Massachusetts Boston

rajini.srikanth@umb.edu

Abstract: In the essay "Why the Solidarity? South Asian Activism for Palestine," Srikanth offers some reasons for the compelling hold of the Palestinian cause on South Asian academics and activists. Referring to India, Pakistan, and Bangladesh in particular, she discusses the extent to which the colonial and neocolonial experiences of these three nations parallel life under Israeli occupation of the Palestinian people. The essay also traces Srikanth's own personal journey of coming into consciousness about Palestine and ties this personal awakening to her role as a teacher.

In *Memory for Forgetfulness*, Darwish's lament and anguished plea for the city of Beirut and the Palestinians living there in exile, he constructs a conversation with the famous Pakistani poet, Faiz Ahmed Faiz:

> [O]ur great friend from Pakistan, Fayiz Ahmad Fayiz, is busy with another question: "Where are the artists?"
>
> "Which artists, Fayiz?" I ask.
>
> "The artists of Beirut."
>
> "What do you want from them?"
>
> "To draw this war on the walls of the city."
>
> "What's come over you?" I exclaim. "Don't you see the walls tumbling?" (*Memory for Forgetfulness*, 65)[1]

Fayiz, or Faiz, as his name is more commonly spelled, lived in self-exile in Beirut from 1979 to 1982, where he edited *Lotus*, the publication of the Afro-Asian Writers' Union. (Faiz left Pakistan to escape the oppressive leadership of President Zia Al-Huq.) The calamitous and destructive bombing of Beirut in August, 1982, led Faiz to write the poem (in Urdu) "For the Palestinian Martyrs," whose concluding lines read:

> Wherever I unfurl
>
> The banner of my blood,
>
> There flutters the flag of Palestine.

Rajini Srikanth is Associate Professor of English and director of the Honors Program at UMass Boston. Her research and teaching explore the intersections of literature and politics. She is deeply committed to the idea of global citizenship, stressing in her writings and teachings the need for a thoughtful, attentive, and responsible engagement with "unfamiliar" histories, cultures, and geographies. Srikanth specializes in Asian American Literature, Native American Writing, literature of the American South, South Asian Diaspora; Race; and theories of pedagogy. She is author of *The World Next Door: South Asian American Literature and the Idea of America* (Temple UP, 2004); *White Women in Racialized Spaces: Imaginative Transformation and Ethical Action in Literature* (SUNY Press, 2002); and *Bold Words: A Century of Asian American Writing* (Rutgers UP, 2001).

One Palestine has been destroyed

By my enemies

But my agony has given birth

To Innumerable Palestines.[2]

Faiz is among numerous South Asian writers, scholars, and activists who find the predicament of the Palestinian people profoundly disturbing. In 1947, when the British left South Asia after 200 years of their presence and colonial rule, the Indian subcontinent was torn in two, and the nations of India and Pakistan were born (and, further, in 1971, Bangladesh was engendered out of East Pakistan). These births were fraught with bloodshed and slaughter. Partition, as the 1947 event signaling the emergence of two nations is known, was accompanied by dislocation and division along religious lines, with many hundreds of thousands of people moving in either direction of an arbitrarily drawn geographical boundary. The devastating deaths accompanying Partition, the loss of property, the breakup of families, with some members remaining on one side of the border and others on the opposite side, are traumas of such magnitude that even today, 62 years later, memories of that horrific time haunt the two nations. Likewise, the birth of Bangladesh in 1971 was a bloody rupture of the Bengali-speaking Pakistanis from their largely Urdu speaking compatriots in the western part of the nation.

The loss of homes, the shock of a life pulverized—these are the actual and inherited experiences that preoccupy large numbers of South Asians. Bollywood and independent films revisit the legacy of Partition (e.g., in the films *Veer Zaara*, *Ghoom Tana*, *LOC Kargil*, *Dhoop*, and *Ramchand Pakistani*), a testament to the enduring hold of this defining moment in the recently decolonized nations' lives. Perhaps the nearness of this history in our collective conscious-

ness is the reason that South Asians are drawn to the struggles of the Palestinian peoples.

Or it may be the experience of colonization and then decolonization. Perhaps the Palestinians are a compelling reminder of what can happen when an erstwhile colonizer leaves a messy political situation behind. The Palestinians are the visible and everyday evidence of injustice endorsed and accepted by the majority of the international community and transmuted into international approbation. And this acquiescence to injustice by numerous governments stands as an affront to many South Asians, who remember in their muscles and bones what it means to be coerced to leave one's home and land. But let me caution that I am not suggesting an exact parallel between the postcolonial situations of India/Pakistan and the circumstances of present-day Palestine. When the British left the Middle East in 1948, not only did they leave behind a situation of unimaginable turmoil by neglecting to articulate clearly the political rights of Palestinians, but also they and the governments of the West implicitly anointed the state of Israel the new colonizer, giving to it the kind of international legitimacy and latitude in its seizure of erstwhile Palestinian territory that was denied the Palestinians, hundreds of thousands of whom had fled their homes during the Israeli attack and longed to return to their, in many cases, ancestral dwellings. The neo-colonialisms that Pakistan (tied as it is to United States' dictates) and India (becoming embroiled in the economic net of global market economies and moving away from its previous proudly held non-aligned status to closer economic and political dependency/ cooperation with the United States) find themselves ensnarled in are of a different kind altogether than the neocolonialism that the Palestinians suffer. The Palestinian people are in the grip of the occupying force of the Israelis – as evidenced by the settlers in the Occupied Territories and the checkpoints and the panoptic surveillance of every aspect of Palestinian life. Thus, when I point to the resonance for South Asians of the unfortunate fallout from imperial practices that the Palestinians suffer, I don't mean to gloss over specific differences. The commonality of experience lies in this: imperial and colonial powers have decided (with disdain and superficial understanding) the fate of South Asians and Palestinians.

However, despite having spent the first 19 years of my life in India and having been born only 10 years after the nation's independence, my recognition of kinship with the Palestinian people was late. Palestine was the hole in my knowing, the question I didn't even know I had to ask, the domain of knowledge that I didn't realize existed. So total was my ignorance, growing up as I did in Bombay (now Mumbai) in a U.S.-centric context in the expatriate community (as one of the few privileged "local" families) of the multinational oil company Esso in the 1960s, that I had no knowledge of the predicament of the Palestinian people. When I first stumbled upon Palestine, viewing the photographs of refugee camps at an exhibition in another Indian city, Bangalore, the shame I felt was necessarily humbling. It made me realize the extent of my ignorance and forced me to acknowledge the unacceptability and inexcusability of my intellectual vacuum. That was when I realized that education can provide darkness as well as illumination. I knew a great deal about the founding of the state of Israel. But I knew nothing of the associated narrative of the Palestinian people. I lived in India, but like many westernized Indians, I was socialized into a particular way of being and knowing that privileged a European and American world view. The school I went to had been set up for expatriate Americans, so it is no surprise that though one colonizer had left India, my consciousness was colonized by a new power.

In the last 15 years, I have had a bracing education in what it means to understand the suffering and the resistance of the Palestinian people. Growing in complexity as an educator, I have learned to listen for silent narratives, to probe the shadows of images hidden in the corners. I have learned to read history as I read the classroom—attentive to the smallest nuance in my students' tones, their posture as they speak with me or with one another, the questions they pose and responses they make to the readings. It is not that my prior indoctrination into support for Israel has been simply replaced by indoctrination into support for Palestinians and their longing for a homeland; it is, rather, that I see now the seductive power of language and the politics of the dissemination of information. The challenge lies in attempting to escape the unstoppable avalanche of anti-Palestinian rhetoric in the mainstream U. S. media. For the most part, even among those who are fierce activists against injustice of all kinds, thinking critically and fighting for justice stops at the Palestinian situation. This is why people like my friend R do what they do.

R is my fearless South Asian friend. She speaks her mind, pursues her causes, and has a clear and lucid understanding of what's fair and just. She tells me a story that I marvel at, because it stands in contrast to my own careful and cautious approach to things. R believes that the times call for a bold declaration of principles. She may sound unattractively militant, but R is a person of unshakable integrity. I, on the other hand, with my restraint, could be guilty of silent complicity; or so it would appear to someone like R. On a recent bus trip from New York to Boston, R is with her partner, Matt.[3] Two young women board the bus with, as she describes it, their "Israel birthright" T-shirts. They are young, enthusiastic, eager and flush with the memories of their recent trip to the "ancestral homeland." R is outraged: she imagines the

Palestinians who cannot return, the residents of refugee camps in Lebanon and Jordan and in the Occupied Territories, and she cannot keep silent. So she begins to talk, loudly so as to be heard, addressing herself to Matt. "Isn't it interesting that some people can go visit a homeland whereas those whose homes were once there cannot even return?" She makes other observations in the same vein. R does not tell me what reaction she gets from the women, whether they even realize that they are the target of her commentary. I don't ask, because I am imagining whether R would have dared such open critique if Matt had not been white, if he had looked obviously Arab. I don't mean to doubt R's courage, but I wonder to what extent Matt's white body serves as a shield. Even as I admire what she does, and I say so to her, I want to ask, as well: "Would you have been so vocal if Matt had looked like a Mansoor?" There is also the part of me that wonders whether this approach, where we instruct through creating discomfort, is necessarily the most productive or constructive mode of engaging those whom we wish to jolt into introspection and examination of their hitherto un-interrogated practices. R's tactic is harsh, and it could in the long-term prove a powerful tool in tearing away the young women's romanticized veil, but it could also cause them to become further ensconced in their unquestioning and sentimental attachment to the state of Israel.

When I relate R's story to my activist and anti-Occupation Israeli friend, she tells me that ignorance can be deliberately cultivated; one can choose not to know, and one can consciously adopt such a stance as a very young person. She did, she says. She was 10 years old when many Palestinian families around her were dispossessed. She could have absorbed more of the reality of their pain, but she chose not to. She observed it clinically, dispassionately, almost as though it were a scene unfolding in her midst to which she had no connection. She

is still struggling, almost 50 years later, with her complicated and entangled emotions, loving the Israeli homeland for what it offers to the Jewish people, deeply critical of it for what it does to the Palestinians. It was she who told me about the "everyday indignities" the Palestinians have to endure; the slow gradual wearing away of their self-respect, the inexorable chipping away of dignity.

Careful, says my Palestinian friend. The issue is not simply one of restoring dignity. Don't forget the political questions that form the foundation of any self-dignity. I recognize the truth of what she says. One can become seduced into self-approbation simply by being respectful to individuals, recognizing their humanity, and paying homage to their personhood. But this self-approbation can be an end point in itself. It can fail to deliver on the truly urgent issues of power and political and civil rights. The return of property. The creation of conditions for economic sovereignty. The right to self-rule. The right to decide one's own fate. My Palestinian friend reminds me that it is not sufficient merely to be treated with dignity and humanity. More important and more critical is the difficult and complex acknowledgement that Israelis need to make to themselves to recognize the ways in which they have systematically denuded the basic fundamental political right of self-determination of the Palestinian people. In most "research" situations that bring Israelis and Palestinians in face-to-face encounters, the emphasis is on the psychological interpersonal dimension; there is little attention paid to the asymmetrical power relationship between the two groups and the fundamental political reality of Israeli privilege and Palestinian disenfranchisement. (See, in this regard, Ramzi Suleiman's essay "Jewish-Palestinian Relations in Israel").[4] Until the asymmetry of power is recognized and acknowledged by the Israelis, and the intersection of the psychological and political realms enabled, the situation is not likely to improve for the Palestinians. Treating your neighbor with dignity requires you to accept his/her desire for self-determination, requires you to interrogate yourself to see whether and how you have impeded her/his right to civil and political liberties and economic and social justice. Every person is entitled to certain rights as a result of his/her humanity; therefore, "rights-holders" presume the existence of "duty-bearers," individuals whose duty it is *not to prevent* the attainment of these rights.[5] At a psychological level, each of us has the capacity to execute the duty of recognizing another person's humanity and claim to rights. This intimate psychological bond between the rights-holder and the duty-bearer provides the foundation on which the edifice of law and political structures can be erected to fulfill the rights of an entire people.

My Palestinian friend mourns the loss of the fierce nationalist spirit that animated those of her father's generation, their hope and aspiration for an independent Palestine crushed. She cannot bear to see the resignation in the elders, the capitulation to the harsh trajectory of circumstances. I listen to her and I wonder how she can persevere in what she does—believing in and working for the future of her people. She said once, "Palestine cannot remain just an idea; it has to become a reality" or words to that effect. I am reminded of what another dear South Asian friend once said, "There are good nationalisms and there are bad nationalisms." Fanon's distrust of the nationalism of newly decolonized nations notwithstanding, I have to concur with my friend that the struggle for a Palestinian state is necessary; it is imperative, because it is about a reclamation of that which was taken away unjustly and it is about returning to one's rightful home.

Nationalism is a complicated notion. Some people in India argue that India is an artificially constructed nation. We were, they say, a collection of many princely states before the British arrived; to force the idea of a single national identity on such a diverse mix of cultural and linguistic groups is untenable, and sooner or later the country will unravel. However, as historian Ramachandra Guha has argued, it is precisely India's recognition of its multiple cultural centers and diverse linguistic practices that has enabled it to survive as a nation more than 60 years after the British departed. Regionalism is as potent a force in India as nationalism, with the regions being carved out largely along linguistic lines. But a national identity is a powerful source of coherence in the face of external threat and oppression. Thus, when my friend and colleague spoke about "good nationalisms" he was differentiating between the nationalism of superpowers with their hegemonic aspirations and those of embryonic and aspiring states that wish to realize their basic right to self-governance and reclaim the resources that have been usurped. Nationalism for Palestinians is about the right to return to their own homes and to their land, and to govern these according to their best interests as a people *without interference and impediment*. South Asians recognize this kind of nationalist aspiration. It resonates profoundly for us.

When we South Asian academics and activists invest passionately in the cause of the Palestinian people, we run the risk of being perceived as appropriating someone else's pain and trauma to give meaning to our lives. But we are not ambulance chasers seeking to aggrandize ourselves in "doing right" for others. Instead, like the Indians in South Africa who belonged to the African National Congress and fought side by side with the black South Africans against the apartheid state, we feel the hunger for homeland of the Palestinian people and understand their outrage at the turmoil left behind by imperial powers playing fast and loose with their lives and desires. How else can we explain Faiz's poem? How else explain Pakistani American Tahira Naqvi's short story "Thank God for the Jews"?[6] How else can we explain the impassioned monologue of the Bangladeshi American young man, Rizwan, in Sharbari Ahmed's play "Raisins Not Virgins" who leaves New York for the Occupied Territories and decides he cannot return:

> I wish I could explain everything to you. Once you've seen what I have, you can't just go back to the past. There are no men over fourteen left in the camp. Soldiers just come and take them away. And the ones left behind, they have nothing left distinguishing them as men, except, well…that, and what the hell good is it anymore? And the checkpoints, […] That's what people don't know about. The humiliation, the true nature of the oppression is played out at those checkpoints. Women and men not allowed to go to work, children not allowed to go to school. Little girls leered at and taunted with guns, little boys challenged unfairly to prove their manhood. I can't come back. I can't live the way I did, insulated and soft. […] The other day I asked an Israeli doctor—his name is Ben—what I could actually do. And he said, "pay attention, and be useful." It occurred to me that's really what anyone should try to do in this world. So, that's what I am doing. I have my eyes open now and I am trying very hard to be useful. I work with Israeli doctors who come into the camps every day and take care of the wounded children.[7]

For me, teaching about the Palestinian situation is a moral obligation. To do it in a way that my students perceive as a genuine invitation to explore and examine their own perspectives is a pedagogical obligation. It is, in the final analysis, a human obligation.

In his poem "I Talk Too Much," Darwish gives voice to this human obligation. He poses a challenge to his readers/listeners: *"Is it true, good ladies and gentlemen, that the earth of Man is for all human beings/ as you say? In that case, where is my little cottage, and where am I?"* (13).[8] It is a compelling question to ask, because this desire for home, this need for a place to call one's own is universally human. I have found it to be the most effective way to introduce students of all backgrounds to the discussion of the Palestinian question. They are outraged that one can be forcibly removed from one's home and not allowed to return. They understand the human rights violation of such an act. And so, when Darwish says, "We travel like everyone else, but we return to nothing" (11)[9], he underscores both the commonality of Palestinians with all other peoples *and* the poignant separateness of their current "homeless" and stateless condition.

ENDNOTES

1. University of California Press, 1995.
2. Translated by Daud Kamal. The translation was given to me by Faiz's niece, Farida Ahmed.
3. Matt is a pseudonym.
4. See, for instance, chapter 2 "Theories of Human Rights" in Jack Donnelly, *International Human Rights* 3rd Edition (Westview Press, 2005), 21-35. Ramzi Suleiman, "Jewish-Palestinian Relations in Israel: The Planned Encounter as a Microcosm." In *Israeli and Palestinian Identities in Dialogue: The School for Peace Approach.* Ed. Rahah Halabi. Rutgers University Press, 2000. 31-47.
5. The story can be found in the collection *Dying in a Strange Country* (Toronto: TSAR Publications, 2001).
6. Sharbari Ahmed's play has been performed several times in New York and Boston. It is currently available as an unpublished manuscript.
7. Mahmoud Darwish, *Unfortunately it was Paradise: Selected Poems.* Trans. and Ed. Munir Akash and Carolyn Forché. University of California Press, 2003.
8. Mahmoud Darwish, "We Travel Like All People." *Unfortunately it was Paradise: Selected Poems.* Trans. and Ed. Munir Akash and Carolyn Forché. University of California Press, 2003.

The Geography of Poetry: Mahmoud Darwish and Postnational Identity

Erica Mena

University of Iowa

ericamena@gmail.com

Abstract: This essay was written several years ago at UMass Boston as part of my Senior Undergraduate Honors Thesis in Literature. Since then, my continued interest in the postnational as a political and social construct has led me to continue examining poetry as a means of accessing ideas of universal community based not on the limited identities of nationality but on chosen affiliations across boundaries of space and time. This was a starting point for a consideration of what arises from post-colonialism from a poetic perspective.

Ours is a country of words: Talk. Talk. Let me rest my road against a stone.

Ours is a country of words: Talk. Talk. Let me see an end to this journey.

(Unfortunately 11)

Mahmoud Darwish, acclaimed as "the saviour of the Arabic Language" (Saith 1), is perhaps today the best known Arabic language poet. Darwish was considered the poet of his people, the Poet Laureate of Palestine, and a voice for the voiceless. His work contains a universality born from specific suffering that reaches across the boundaries of language and nation to "inscribe the national within the universal" (Darwish, *Unfortunately* xix). The dual project of Darwish's work is simultaneously anti-colonial, concerned politically with the establishment of an independent and self-determined Palestine free from imperial occupation, and postnational in the sense that Said hints at in his introduction to *Culture and Imperialism*. Said describes "new alignments made across ... nations" which "provoke and challenge the fundamentally static notion of *identity* that has been the core of cultural thought during the era of imperialism ... by which one is defined by the nation, which in turn derives its authority from a supposedly unbroken tradition" (Said xxv). This gesture beyond identity defined in national terms requires a movement beyond the structures of postcolonial identity.

If post-colonial identity is founded in the anti-colonial establishment of an historical nation, projected linearly through time by means of narrative, postnational identity is loosed from the bonds of causal time. Said takes this point from Eliot's "Tradition

Erica Mena is a poet and translator. She completed her BA in English and the Study of Religion at UMass Boston, her M.Phil in Criticism and Culture at the University of Cambridge and is currently pursuing an MFA in Literary Translation at the University of Iowa. Her poetry has appeared with Arrowsmith Press and Pressed Wafer, and is forthcoming in *Dos Passos Review*. Her book of translations of Puerto Rican poet Etnairis Rivera, *Return To The Sea*, was published in 2006. Her translations of Roberto Bolaño's prose poetry are forthcoming in Words Without Borders.

and the Individual Talent" writing:

> "Past and present inform each other, each implies the other and, in the totally idea sense intended by Eliot, each co-exists with the other. What Eliot proposes, in short, is a vision of literary tradition that, while it respects temporal succession, is not wholly commanded by it." (Said 4)

The postnational relies on the destabilization of temporality and territory, and strives to create an identity capable of engagement with universal systems. Contextualizing and demystifying the national narrative, the postnational collapses time from a progressive movement along points on a line into a *momentary eternity,* a "fluid ever-changing present" (Zamorano, 106 in Friberg). In this postnational scape, imagining becomes a kind of agency, constructing oneself, and one's place in the world as well as the possibility for political and cultural interaction and reproduction. This occurs especially through poetry: narrative forms, as context-driven, reproduce cohesive communities, while poetics, as context-generative, produce ruptures leading to new possibilities. It is the postnational and context-generative nature of Darwish's poetry that focuses my reading throughout this paper, which by no means should be understood as minimizing his anti-colonial political agenda, but rather as situating the two moves as simultaneous and mutually informing.

Darwish writes in "I Belong There," "I have learned and dismantled all the words in order to draw from them a single word: *Home*" (*Unfortunately* 7). This statement, as pure in its elegance as it is in its raw desperation, not only speaks to a commonality of suffering but stands (without necessarily demanding) deeper analysis, yielding a richer understanding of the relationship between words and place. It is not the physi-

cal location but the word *"Home"* that the poet has created, and the word has been created only through the destruction of all words. Paradoxically, one assumes the word *"Home"* was among "all the words," and was therefore learned and dismantled along with them, only to be reborn from the understanding of all the words, which is to say all the world. As words are signifiers for the world, so they symbolize what they represent, and from words an understanding of what they represent is created. But it is only by "dismantling" all the words, which is to say the world, that *Home* (and what it signifies) can be found—as the driving motivation behind all action, and that to which everything returns.

Though even that one line could stand deeper explication, its urgent despair for *Home* is readily apparent and universally significant. Rising as it does from Darwish's experience of exile, of homelessness, it addresses not only the Palestinian people's disarticulation (both literally and figuratively), but that of all displaced persons. In "Another Road in the Road"—a title that speaks to the endlessness of the journey of exile—Darwish writes: "I am from here, I am from there, yet am neither here nor there" (*Unfortunately* 4). The physical displacement in the last phrase does not diminish the place of origin in the first clause ("I am from here"). This seems at first glance to be only within the concerns of the post-colonial exile literary tradition. While the establishment of a physical Palestinian nation is a central concern for Darwish within his work, it is no less his concern to establish concomitantly a community that moves beyond geography and nation. Darwish said: "I want, both as a poet and as a human being, to free myself from Palestine. But I can't. When my country is liberated, so shall I be" (Saith 1). Darwish's Palestine is a memory, an imagined nation in the truest form.

Exile literature may be categorized as a part of the post-colonial literary tradition because of the shared concern with identity in connection to the geography of a nation-state, or lack thereof. While the experience of exile informs Darwish's work, I do not believe Darwish to be primarily an "exile writer." Rather, Darwish is in a sense a postnational writer—his postnationality is one of necessity, rather than explicit choice, because by necessity Darwish creates and expresses a community that is without national borders.

Darwish is not given the choice to look beyond his nation, but rather by necessity of circumstance carries his community with him as an imagined construct. He is thus able to write beyond the constraints of the borders of national identity, and reach a community of people who are external to any sense of "Palestinian-ness." Where the post-colonial literary tradition is primarily concerned with a re-establishment of displaced identity through connection to land, the postnational is concerned with moving beyond the need for a primary connection to boundaries. Darwish does this inherently, in part because his circumstance as a Palestinian does not allow for anything else.

The post-colonial sense of time is one of progression: from a projected historical narrative to an infinitely extending future, the post-colonial nation posits a fixed causal beginning and no end. The postnational community, however, exists in a cyclical time, when past and future exist simultaneously and are interconnected in a momentary eternity. Here, it is important to keep in mind the difference between the postnational *community* and the abstract *nation*; the nation, even in a wholly abstract form, still relies on temporal boundaries to define it and oppose itself against.

Darwish's work illustrates this postnational sense of time. "An end like a beginning, like the beginning of an end" Darwish writes in "The Hoopoe" (*Unfortunately* 35), and later *Everything will begin again*" in "The Lute of Ismael" (*Unfortunately* 66).

The end is a beginning, and has a beginning. It is not a fixed movement from one to the other, but they are similar and connected through. Later, in "The Owl's Night" Darwish uses a refrain-like phrase that explores the shifting of this momentary eternity:

> There is, here, a present not embraced
> by the past.
> When we reached the last of the trees,
> we knew we were unable to pay
> attention.
> And when we returned to the ships, we
> saw absence piling up its chosen
> objects
> and pitching its eternal tent around us.
> …
> There is, here, a timeless present, and
> here no one can find anyone.
> No one remembers how we went out
> the door like a gust of wind,
> and at what hour we fell from
> yesterday, and then
> yesterday shattered on the tiles
> in shards for others to reassemble into
> mirrors
> reflecting their images over ours.
>
> There is, here, a placeless present.
> Perhaps I can handle my life and cry
> out in the owl's night:
> *Was this condemned man my father who*
> *burdens me with his history?*
> Perhaps I will be transformed within
> my name, and will choose
> my mother's words and way of life,
> exactly as they should be.
> …
> There is, here a transient present.
> (63-64)

The present shifts through the poem, first disconnected from the past in a separateness that arrives to unity as the present becomes "placeless" and "transient." This shift exemplifies the shift into postnationality. At first the present is "not embraced by the past"—the two cannot be reconciled. The present is projected back onto the past to force an agreement between the two, which necessarily distorts both. The inability to pay attention and the "absence piling up its chosen objects" could be read as this distortion of the past under the lens of post-colonial identity. The "eternal tent" closes the poet off from the world, surrounding the poet and his readers in the historical imagination of national identity. This is the border of the abstract nation—its existence in time. While the physical nation imposes itself on geography, drawing borders and boundaries, the abstract nation is born and lost in time. In the postnational reality however, time is not a series of causes and effects, nor a linear progression, but a constant flux. It is precisely this that is the "momentary eternity"—rather than projecting a fixed linear progression both backwards and forwards in time from the present, each moment of the present is taken individually as reality, and as a constantly shifting experience. The sense of the present in the poem shifts and becomes "timeless," without progression or change which erases the past. Darwish writes that "no one can find anyone," that they "fell from yesterday"—they are unable to even form a community in this "timeless present" that is cut off from its past, both literally because of the suppression of the Palestinian history, and metaphorically because of the drive towards continuity that erases the historical reality of the past.

There is an insular sense of the post-colonial present as timeless that separates individuals from their community and from their past as well. Because in a post-colonial sense of history, the present national independence is projected as a pre-colonial condition, and also as an inevitably continuous future condition, there is a sense of the timelessness, the unchangingness, of the post-colonial reality. Post-coloniality requires this timelessness in order to assert its national authority over identity, claiming that the national identity as defined in the post-colonial period always existed, was imposed upon by the condition of being a colony, but has been recovered and will always exist. In this sense the timelessness amounts to unchangingness tied to place. However, in each repetition in the poem the present is "here," a word emphasized by the commas on either side of it. It is a present connected to *space*, and in the third repetition we come to that postnational movement: "There is, here, a placeless present." It is here, but it is placeless, which is to say it is physically existent but not limited to place. Once the present is freed from the necessity of projecting itself into the past, creating a continuous linear progression up to itself, it can also move beyond the ties to place. Only then can the poet reach beyond the present and the past to his connection with his family, his community, his "mother's words and way of life, exactly as they should be."

Darwish's postnationality is one of necessity. Because the post-colonial condition requires a connection to land and historical place that the Palestinian people have not been able to realize, they are by circumstance both a colonized nation and a postnational community. Post-coloniality therefore is a mis-categorization of Darwish; his writing is significantly concerned with building a community that is independent of national borders and outside of linear historical progression in order to enact simultaneous anti-colonial and postnational agendas. It is extra-temporal, and existing only through language it is both eternal and changing, rather than the static infinite projected by the post-colonial nation.

This complex relationship with time is one that is difficult to relate in English, and within the constraints of Western literary theory, but is vital to understanding Darwish's poetry.[1] He returns to it in "Ivory Combs:"

Would that I had a different present,
I would hold the keys to my past.
And would that I had a past within me,
I would possess all tomorrows.
...
Here is the obsession with a song
through which I convey a repeated
tragedy. (79-80)

The present as it is (the postnational present) distances the poet from causal history, and therefore the past that is necessary as a cause of the future. The relationship is interwoven, but begins not with the past but with the present—for it is from the present that all understanding of past and future come. Following this is a phrase in which the poet becomes the singer and storyteller, historian, prophet and teacher. Darwish is conveying the "repeated tragedy" of not only his experience, and the Palestinian people's experience, but that of anyone who has been displaced either spatially, linguistically or temporally.

Throughout Darwish's work this question of identity in the face of displacement continues to be a primary one. This concern with identity, however, is not one that looks simply to reconnect a specific identity claim with corresponding borders, linguistic or geographic, but one that seeks to answer more abstract questions about developing an identity rooted in community as constructed through words, or rather, through what the words represent.

Who am I? This is a question that others ask, but has no answer.

---

[1] "Further, because Arabic has no tense as such, grammatical time is not, as in English, defined in relation to the moment of speech, a process that interjects an implied subject in every utterance. Arabic prose does not have to maintain the consistent pattern of tense sequence required in English. Hence it is easy for Darwish to scramble time, removing the action from the temporal sphere and placing it in a dreamlike realm" (Darwish, *Memory for Forgetfulness* xxvii).

I am my language. ...
I am my language. I am words' writ:
    Be! Be my body!
...
No land on earth bears me. Only my
    words bear me,
...
This is my language, a necklace of stars
    around the necks
of my loved ones. They emigrated.
They carried the place and emigrated,
    they carried the time and
    emigrated.
...
We don't linger upon what is to come.
There is no tomorrow in this desert,
    save what we saw yesterday,
so let me brandish my ode to break the
    cycle of time,
and let there be beautiful days!
How much past tomorrow holds! (90-92)

Without linear history and place there is only language connecting community. Darwish writes later in the poem: "This is my language, my miracle.../my first identity, my polished metal, the desert idol of an Arab / who worships what flows from rhymes like stars in his *aba*, / and who worships his own words" (*Unfortunately* 93). Language for Darwish is home and self—it is outside of place and time, because with it "they carried the place...they carried the time." This poem exemplifies what Saith wrote about Darwish: "His poetry gives power to the tired and forlorn, to revive, restore, and relive the imagined mobile space called home" (Saith 1). His identity formed from words, portable and untied to a physical nation, is universally experienceable and communicable. It is the identity he is claiming not only for himself, but also for anyone reading his words. However, it is his "first identity," which implies correctly that there are layers and a multiplicity to identity.

Darwish never denies that the establishment of a Palestinian nation is a concern for him; and the development of national identity is part of that establishment. He was a senior officer in the PLO for many years, and continued to be vocal about this issue. But this national identity comes after the "first identity" founded in language, through poetry. Darwish said in an interview: "Poems can't establish a state. But they can establish a metaphorical homeland in the minds of the people. I think my poems have built some houses in this landscape" (Politics of Poetry 1). In "Mural" he writes: "I don't want to return to any country. / After this long absence, I want only to return to my language..." (*Unfortunately* 145). The community constructed through poetry, and the identity based in that community is essential for the poet. In "The Last Train Has Stopped" Darwish asks "Where can I free myself of the homeland in my body?" (*Unfortunately* 15). The desire is to be free of the borders of history and nation, to find an un-colonizable, un-occupiable, lasting source for identity. Later, in "The Hoopoe" he asks: "A boundary within a boundary surrounds us. / What is behind the boundary?" (*Unfortunately* 34). The answer is language, words, poetry. Because his identity exists first in language, outside of the restrictions of time and geography, it is unconquerable, indestructible, and transportable. It is also accessible to those who would be placed outside a community based in national borders, or ethnic heritage. "Denied the recognition of citizenship...Darwish settled on language as his identity, and took upon himself the task of restoration of meaning and thus, homeland" (Darwish, *Unfortunately* xvii). "We have both been freed from the gravity of the land of identity," he writes in "Who Am I, Without Exile?" and the freedom he speaks of is this freedom of self from "the land of identity," the ties to the physical borders of the nation (Darwish, *Unfortunately* 115).

The postnational, though related to the post-colonial, is quite distinct. Postnational communities exist outside of the boundaries of the nation, both the physical borders and the temporal progression that enclose a nation's people. Postnational communities also determine identity by inclusivity, rather than by opposition and exclusivity, and are not limited by linguistic, geographic or historical borders but rather invite all to participate in a collective imagining. Darwish developed a postnational community through his work by necessity. His identity and his community are formed inherently outside of the borders of the nation, but in this location he finds the strength and power of the postnational community equally important to his anti-colonial project.

The poet sees that the adopted, imposed or adapted model of national authority cannot, as Said wrote, merely replace old authority with new authority, but must be transcended in order to establish a truly self-determinate and free community. Darwish is able to do so in large part because of the form he work in. Poetry works to construct postnational identity because it is already outside of the control of causal history and a limited exclusive national experience. This does not mean that it is not rooted in the specific. Rather the different expectations and functions of the form allow the poet to make universally accessible the individual or specific experiences related.

In this way, Darwish is a "poet of the people" (*Unfortunately* xviii) and writes in "Mural:" "I wish to live. I have work to do on this volcanic bit of geography" (*Unfortunately* 139). Though his use of the word "geography" invokes ties to specific national borders, it seems in context to encompass more than just the Palestinian territory. The work that Darwish is referring to is not restricted to the physical borders of geography, but occurs also in the abstract geography of community constructed through poetry. Darwish expresses his obligation towards their community to work, through their words, to be a voice for the voiceless (and to create a state for the stateless, if only in abstraction). Darwish writes later in the same poem: "We—who are capable of remembrance—are capable of liberation" (Darwish, *Unfortunately* 151). It is the poet who remembers for the people, and who makes possible the liberation of his community. In liberating his people, Darwish is also making it possible to develop broader communities. In an interview Darwish said: "The first step of real peace is to know the other side, its culture and creativity" (Omer 2) and in a different context: "Poetry and beauty are always making peace. When you read something beautiful you find coexistence: it breaks walls down" (Saith 2).

WORKS CONSULTED

Anderson, Benedict. *Imagined Communities.* Revised edition. London: Verso, 1991.

Ashcroft, Bill, ed. *The Empire Writes Back.* Second edition. London and New York: Routledge, 2002.

Bhabha, Homi K, ed. *Nation and Narration.* London and New York: Routledge, 1990.

Bhabha, Homi K. *The Location of Culture.* London and New York: Routledge, 2004.

Darwish, Mahmoud. *Unfortunately, It Was Paradise.* Trans. and Ed. Munir Akash and Carolyn Forché with Sinan Antoon and Amira El-Zein. Berkeley, Los Angeles, London: University of California Press, 2003.

Darwish, Mahmoud. *Memory for Forgetfulness.* Trans. Ibrahim Muhawi. Berkeley, Los Angeles, London: University of California Press, 1995.

Darwish, Mahmoud. Interview. *"The Politics of Poetry." Newsweek International.* 20 March 2000: 62. *Thomson Gale.* University of Massachusetts Boston. 29 Oct. 2005. <http://find.galegroup.com.ere-sources.lib.umb.edu/itx/info-mark.do?&type=retrieve&tabID=T002&prodId=EAIM&docId=A60118783&source=gale&userGroup-Name=mlin_b_umass&version=1.0>.

Fanon, Frantz. *The Wretched of the Earth.* New York: Grove Press, 1965.

Habermas, Jürgen. *The Postnational Constellation.* Trans. and ed. Max Pensky. Cambridge: Polity Press, 2001.

Handal, Nathalie. *"Mahmoud Darwish: Palestine's poet of exile." The Progressive* 66.5 (May 2002): 24(3). *Thomson Gale.* University of Massachusetts Boston. 29 Oct. 2005. <http://find.galegroup.com.ere-sources.lib.umb.edu/itx/info-mark.do?&type=retrieve&tabID=T002&prodId=EAIM&docId=A86047772&source=gale&userGroup-Name=mlin_b_umass&version=1.0>.

Lefevere, André. "Composing the Other." *Post-Colonial Translation: Theory and Practice.* Ed. Susan Bassnett, Harish Trivedi. London: Routledge, 1999. 75-94.

Omer, Mohammed. *"Opening a space for jasmine: Mahmoud Darwish, poet of Palestine—and the world." Washington Report on Middle East Affairs* 24.5 (July 2005): 72(2). *Thomson Gale.* University of Massachusetts Boston. 29 Oct. 2005. <http://find.galegroup.com.ere-sources.lib.umb.edu/itx/info-mark.do?&type=retrieve&tabID=T002&prodId=EAIM&docId=A133573562&source=gale&userGroup-Name=mlin_b_umass&version=1.0>.

Said, Edward. *Orientalism.* New York: Vintage Books, 1979.

Said, Edward. *Culture and Imperialism.* New York: Vintage Books, 1994.

Saith, Ashwani. "Mahmoud Darwish: Hope as Home in the Eye of the Storm." *ISIM Review* 15: Spring 2005. 28-29.

Tambini, Damian. "Post-national citizenship." *Ethnic and Racial Studies,* 24:2 (March 2001).

Zamorano Llena, Carmen. "'It's time for some new coinage': Derek Mahon's Redefinition of Identity and the Memory of Place in a Postnational(ist) Context" in *Recovering Memory: Irish Representations of Past and Present.* ed. by Hedda Friberg, Irene Gilsenan Nordin and Lene Yding Pederse. Newcastle: Cambridge Scholars Publishing, 2007.

The Lost and Forgotten: Exploring the Narratives of Darwish and Silko

Kyleen Aldrich

University of Massachusetts Boston

kyleenpa@yahoo.com

Abstract: This essay was written in response to Darwish's book *Memory for Forgetfulness* along with Leslie Marmon Silko's book of stories, *Storyteller*. The author, Kyleen Aldrich, discusses the effects of languages disappearing, the loss of culture, diversity, and knowledge of nature and history. She explores Darwish's book as a work that is seeking liberation through remembering and confronting the past in order to retrieve what is lost by capturing actions with words. Silko and Darwish speak of discrimination, displacement, and exile of a people. Aldrich explicates the importance of memory and shows that by remembering, we recognize what is lost, what can be reclaimed and how writing makes it is possible to preserve these memories. She employs writing as history's witness in these two works. Inspired by the words of Silko and Darwish, the author talks about the common misconception of humans who see one another as separate when we are united by our connection with the land. She asks questions such as while the world is changing, what are we doing to save it? This serves the purpose of calling attention to the warning sent out by Darwish and Silko to all that not enough attention is focused on land and culture and what can potentially be lost.

"And as we move away, we can see ourselves turning into memories. We are these memories. As of this moment, we'll remember each other as we'll remember a distant world disappearing into a blueness more blue than it used to be" (Darwish 60).

So many languages are disappearing. Our knowledge and appreciation of diverse cultures, nature and history are being lost. As time moves on, more and more things are lost.

In *Storyteller* by Leslie Marmon Silko, there is a recurring theme of loss that is subverted as the writing attempts to preserve what is at stake. By telling stories, she tries to keep the memory of the homeland and the tradition of oral culture alive. Her writing advocates cultural endurance and through the stories of Pueblo culture, she creates a clear connection of the people to the land. Silko tells stories about storytelling, to show the culture and its identity. "They passed down an entire culture by word of mouth, an entire history, an entire vision of the world which depended upon memory and retelling by subsequent generations" (Silko 5-6). Oral culture was the story of the people; it was what kept them

Kyleen Aldrich is a junior chemistry major at UMass Boston. She is a member of the honors program as well as the National Society of High School Scholars and the Alpha Lambda Delta branch of UMass Boston; two organizations based on academic merit. Although unsure of her exact career path, she hopes to acquire the skills and necessities to later become a successful pharmacist and enter the medical field, and to also conduct research in the study of Green Chemistry. Her hobbies include reading, writing, and music. Kyleen was first introduced to the works of Mahmoud Darwish in her freshman year of college in Prof. Dorothy Nelson's English 101 class. She participated in the UMass Boston tribute to the life and poetry of Mahmoud Darwish in December 2008.

alive. It is hard to maintain life without culture, because culture *is* a way of life. Silko is transforming an oral culture to one preserved on paper. The reader can trust Silko's words because of the ancestry within them. She was raised by the stories of the Laguna Pueblo culture and she honors the many generations that have passed on in her writing.

A constant battle between memory and forgetfulness is waged in Mahmoud Darwish's book *Memory for Forgetfulness*. His writing serves as a return to the past, a record of one day, of a life, of a cultural identity. I see his work as a memorial to the struggles of the Palestinians, which seek liberation through remembering and confronting the past and retrieving what is lost by capturing actions with words. Darwish states his purpose: "we want to liberate ourselves, our countries, our minds and live in the modern age with competence and pride. In writing, we give expression to our faith in the potency of writing. And we announce further that we are children of this age, and not of the past or the future" (141). He speaks for those who protest in silence, when he says he wants to be remembered, he wants to feel that Beirut exists despite the bombings, and he wants to recover his lost identity that has been swept away by the tides of war.

Both cultures are occupied, physically and mentally. How do the writers break through the barriers of convention? By telling their stories, they try to break free of the stereotypical chains constricting Native Americans and Palestinians. Many of Silko's stories are centered on interdependence of mother and child, which represents the need to take care of the future because their culture is always under attack. An example of this can be seen in Silko's story *Lullaby*. She tells of how "Laguna culture had been irrevocably altered by the European intrusion – —principally by the practice of taking the children away from Laguna to Indian schools, taking the children away from the tellers who had in all past generations told the children, an entire culture, an entire identity of a people" (Silko 6). Though the Americans may have believed that they were 'civilizing' the Indians in these schools, they were destroying their culture. The Indians were forced to speak English and to cut their long, braided hair, resulting in a suppression of their Indian language and traditions. When an Indian returned from fighting in an American war he was changed. Leon, in "Tony's Story," is flabbergasted when Tony kills the white policeman who had been harassing them. Perhaps Indians were seen as savage people for killing the white man, because that was the only way they could prevent the cultural invasion of white supremacy; they were ridding their culture of the 'white devil'. "Americanization" is synonymous with cultural loss.

The Palestinians in Beirut were living in exile after being forced out of Palestine by the Israelis in 1948. They were displaced in camps and became great resistors, refusing to let the Israelis justify their cruelty. Americans were behind the scenes, aiding Israel – —the perpetrators of the Beirut siege. Darwish observed that being white was "something more precious than freedom itself" (98). He speaks in the voice of an oppressor when he says, "these Palestinians are not human. They're animals who walk on all fours" (77). In response to this racism, Darwish reasons that, "he has to strip us of our humanity to justify killing us, for the killing of animals – —unless they're dogs – —is not forbidden in Western law" (77). But when we see what is being done, who is really the animal?

Stories about loss are not considered happy tales. Silko and Darwish speak of discrimination, displacement, and exile of a people. But is it wrong to tell 'bad' stories? We should not obliterate chunks of history simply because they do not exemplify the good deeds of man. Telling a 'bad' story is not malicious, because all stories matter.

What is malicious is trying to hide parts of history. Leaving out something would be like telling the truth, but not the whole truth. In the words of the old man in *Storyteller*, "It will take a long time, but the story must be told. There must not be any lies" (Silko 26). People who have written history have altered it; there is always a struggle to tell the whole truth. In *Storyteller*, the woman in the story has killed a man, and she is promised she will be set free from jail if she says he "just fell through the ice." But she does not lie; she knows she killed him. Lying would change the story and she had learned this from the old man who "would not change the story even when he knew the end was approaching. Lies could not stop what was coming" (Silko 32). And lies cannot change history. Silko's stories switch back and forth from good to bad, but that is the point she is trying to make. She is giving us the whole picture, not just what we want to hear. The bad stories shed light on the possibility of a better life for all. The idea of transformation and its healing powers found in many of Silko's stories inspires the belief that change can bring about something good from something bad.

When I first read Silko's *Yellow Woman*, it sounded like a 'bad' story. She had been kidnapped by Buffalo Man, was far away from home, raped, and forced to journey all the way back home alone. Yes, these things are bad, but did good come out of it? I came to realize that Yellow Woman was not hurt by these experiences. She had forgotten her past and was trapped by her culture, and in the story you can see a change; she needed the experience to learn what the past means to her culture. When Buffalo Man left, she was free to go if she wanted, but she chose to stay; it wasn't kidnapping anymore. What we see in society in a negative way tends to be strictly labeled as a bad thing, but in Silko's stories these principles are reversed. It is important to open our eyes to more than one side of life and to awaken to a deeper understanding of the world. We

need all the stories to avoid isolation of people and events; in this way we create collective memory.

Our culture tends to erase bad moments in history, or at least, we try to forget them. This kind of amnesia is prevalent in the U.S. Why is this? Is it because we don't want to remember ourselves in a bad light? What would happen if we tried to forget the history we don't want to remember? Would that erase its existence? Darwish writes about the bombing of Hiroshima and says, "what I remember of Hiroshima is the American attempt to make it forget its name" (Darwish 84). The Americans tried to bomb it out of existence, along with its people. But by doing so, they created memory, and we cannot cover up the wrongs done to a country with flowers over graves of those who lost their names. Darwish feels that Americans don't care about Palestine. Do Americans care about Indians? Do we address these terrible wrongs committed against them? Is it racism that makes us act this way?

There were numbers of people who died in the bombings of Hiroshima who cannot be recovered, but math cannot account for loss. Can language account for loss? If our society tries to hide the bad things, then why is our media only plagued by stories of disease, racism, violence, and death? These stories have lost their meaning in the world today. Death is talked about in the news and is given no more speculation, causes no more grief, and heeds no more importance than what the weather will be like tomorrow. Will making a quick reference to the deaths of thousands of people in the newspaper make up for it?

We need to remember. By remembering, we create recognition of what is lost, recognition of what can be reclaimed; we are saving by witnessing the past. Can we make up for the mistakes of the past by letting its stories be told? We keep the stories for those who come after us, but more importantly, we keep the stories for those who were before us, so that we may remember them, and cry for them.

Do we write, then, to preserve the memories? Darwish says, "it is galling that we should be ready during these air raids to steal time for all this chatter, defending the role of the poet whose writing is unique because it is rooted in his relationship to the actual as it unfolds, that we should be doing this at a moment in which everything has stopped talking, a moment of shared creativity when the people's epic is shaping its own history" (Darwish 64). He implies that the people themselves are the memory. If that is so, what happens when the people die? Does the memory die too? Perhaps this is why we must write. If there are no people, who will tell the story? Writing is history's witness. It unites what is separated, creates poetry from silence, and memory from words.

Writing itself is under siege in these books, as much as Beirut. I see writing as an attempt to revitalize language, but the poets struggle for the right language. What is the right language? Darwish asks, "What is poetry? Poetry is to write this cosmic silence, final and total" (Darwish 154). Does silence hide language? Poetry exists, even if it is not being written, it is still there. But can poetry actually capture in words what is taking place? If history cannot speak for itself, these memoirs will. These authors tell the story of the cruelty and slavery towards Indians and Palestinians, but "anybody can act violently – —there is nothing to it; but not every person is able to destroy his enemy with words" (Silko 222). Silko and Darwish are striking back with their words, releasing them to the world, and exposing their oppression.

In Silko's stories, we learn about the Pueblo culture and its issues. But she is not just writing for the benefit of indigenous peoples, she is writing to inform the West of new ways of knowing, hoping to break the barrier of conventionalism and stereotypes. We need new ethics that focus on what matters, what has been lost and what needs to be found. We learn from the Native Americans in Silko's stories of the interconnectedness of all things. Aunt Susie's stories depict transformations between humans and nature, humans and animals, little girls and butterflies. Silko and Darwish point out the common misconception of humanity; that we see ourselves as separate from each other, but we can come together, if we so choose to see the connection of us all with the land.

In these stories, the people are part of the land, and attached to it. The Palestinians living in Beirut are being told to leave, are being murdered in great numbers, but they cannot leave. The Native Americans live with the land, the earth is their mother, the sky is their father, and the winds are their brothers, and they are together always in life and in death (Silko 51). The purpose of these stories is to remember land. Is it possible that one can live in a place for ten years and still not know it or their existence in it, like Darwish, because it has changed?

Land is being changed, and it is being destroyed. I feel that Silko's stories are a signal that "drastic things must be done for the world to continue" (Silko 65). While the world is changing, what are we doing to save it? I believe Darwish and Silko want to do more than just preserve the memory of the land they remember; they want to save it, and fight for it. Darwish and Silko send out a warning to the people who do not pay enough attention to land and culture. The bear made of ice is coming and we are gradually losing our grip of the earth, as we are too busy waging a war against ourselves, destroying nature and culture in the process, all the while strengthening separation.

WORKS CITED

Darwish, Mahmoud. *Memory For Forgetfulness: August, Beirut, 1982*. University of California Press: Berkeley and Los Angeles, California, 1995.

Silko, Leslie M. *Storyteller*. Arcade Publishing: New York, 1981.

An Anthem for the Dream Land

The Legacy of Poetry for the Palestinian and African-American Nationalism in the 1960s and 1970s

Nadia Alahmed

University of Massachusetts Amherst

nalahmed@complit.umass.edu

Abstract: The article is an introduction to a larger project seeking comparisons in origin, ideology, aesthetics and political agendas of two artistic movements: The Black Arts Movement and the Palestinian Culture of Resistance, in 1960s and 1970s. The Bandung Conference in 1955 and the rise of the anti-colonial movement in Algiers and Africa in the 1950-1960s shaped the establishment of the Third World Movement, which brought forth the rise of radical political and literary nationalism in the Occupied Territories and within the African-American community. This research is an attempt to reveal the resemblance between these political ideologies and their formative impact on the political consciousness and literary expression of these two peoples. With poetry as its primary focus, the article elucidates similarities in the literary traditions, mythology and aesthetics that united African-American and Palestinian poetry in the 1960-70s in their struggle for self-determination, sovereignty and global justice.

"We have a country of words. Speak speak so I can put my road on the stone of a stone. We have a country of words. Speak speak so we may know the end of this travel." —Mahmoud Darwish, "We Travel Like All Other People"

I. INTRODUCTION

The 1960s and 1970s appear as a symbol of revolution in the African-American history and stand out as a period of a crucial ideological, political and cultural change in Palestinian history as well. The decade brought about revolutions of numerous kinds and various levels all around the globe, but a specific political phenomenon holds the most profound impact in the political consciousness of African Americans and the Palestinian community alike. The decolonization movement with the rise of what Frantz Fanon called "consciousness of the colonized" and the Third World Movement became raw material for the new Palestinian and African-American political agendas, saturated with revolutionary and nationalist ideas.

The major event that is thought to have inspired the anti-colonial movement is the Afro-Asian conference held in 1955 in Bandung, Indonesia. It is the first example of active collaboration between the Third World countries that manifested their will to struggle for sovereignty and equality of all nations and races. A few years after the

Nadia Alahmed is a Ph.D. student at the Department of Comparative Literature at the University of Massachusetts, Amherst. Her interests include 20th century African-American, Palestinian and Slavic (Russian and Ukrainian) literature, concentrating on the revolutionary artistic movements of the 1960s and 1970s. She is actively researching historical and literary connections between these literatures and seeks to discover the ways in which political circumstances interact with artistic creations.

conference all the ideals of Bandung were brought to life as the world was witnessing the rise of new independent nations and the intensive process of decolonization throughout the Third World. Just two years after the event, in 1957, Ghana became the first African nation to gain independence from the British Empire. Ghana's Leader, Kwame Nkrumah, affirmed his position as a major figure in the anti-colonialist movement and became the leader of the first independent African nation. Another leader of liberation and nationalist struggles arose when Gamal Abdel Nasser became the first democratic leader of Egypt in 1956. Nasser not only encouraged a great number of uprisings and liberation struggles in various places on the African continent but also brought about the rebirth of the Arab nationalist ideology, which culminated in the creation of the Arab League in 1964. By 1970s each and every North African country became a member of this organization.

In 1962 the Algiers gained independence fulfilling the life-long dream of Frantz Fanon, a prominent Black scholar and psychologist from Martinique, who made a profound contribution to the anti-colonization and anti-racist struggles in Algeria and throughout the African continent. At this point it is difficult to ignore the strength of historical connections between Arab and African nationalisms and political struggles. Where does the Middle East or Arab World end and Africa begin? Do countries like Egypt, Algiers, and Morocco, as well as other Muslim and Arabic speaking countries on the African continent belong among the African nations or do they embody the Pan Arab ideals of Nasser and constitute a part of the Arab world? It is not my intent here to provide the answers to either one of these complex questions. My focus rather is to reveal the connections between African and Arab nationalisms and the struggle for self-determination and dignity, using the example of African-American community and the Palestinian people, each of whom

without a doubt made an enormous contribution to these struggles. In many ways, the African American and Palestinian Diasporas created by exile and displacement, as well as the Palestinian people under occupation and the ones living within Israeli borders, provide a powerful link between the vast territories of Middle Eastern and African continents and the Western world through their cultural and political activism.

I am obliged to emphasize the enormous scope of work embedded in a proper survey of my thesis and affirm that this article is only a brief introduction to a much larger project dedicated to African American/Palestinian collaboration and similar tendencies in their political and aesthetic ideologies. I also acknowledge that my analysis is not historical, but rather political, artistic and cultural, even though political background is essential to understanding of both Black Arts Movement and the Palestinian Culture of Resistance.

II. ARTISTIC MOVEMENTS IN COMPARATIVE HISTORICAL CONTEXT

It is a difficult task to define a clear historical framework for an artistic movement, and the Black Arts Movement is not an exception. Nevertheless, its emergence is connected to the assassination of Malcolm X in 1965 and poet and playwright Amiri Baraka's coming to Harlem to fulfill the deceased leader's dream of establishing a center for Black Arts. Consequently, Baraka became one of the key figures in the Black Arts Movement and shaped many ideological and political characteristics of the Black artistic struggle for justice and self-determination, contributing to the transformation of "Arts" into a "Movement." A year later, in1966, Ghassan Kanafani, a prominent Palestinian poet, writer, and politician for the first time applied the term "resistance" to Palestinian literature (Harlow, 5). Kanafani coined a concept delineating the major literary movement in the Palestinian literature, creating a solid ground not only for the literary mode of resistance, but also for establishing and affirming the entire phenomenon understood as the Palestinian Culture of Resistance.

In order to trace the historical development of the Black Arts Movement and the Palestinian Culture of Resistance, it is necessary to take a closer look at the Palestinian and Afro-American historical standpoint at that time.

The African-American community along with the oppressed Palestinian population were profoundly influenced by the anti-colonization struggles exploding everywhere in the Third World. Malcolm X emphasized the crucial necessity for the sovereignty of African Americans and the unity with African nations, and made an enormous impact on the African American political consciousness. Nationalist ideas, as well as the revival of African heritage and the connections with the African countries, became the creed and political goal of Black Artists. The 1960s-1970s was a crucial period in the history of Palestinian nationhood and political consciousness as well. The Palestinian political ideology became imbued with radical nationalist ideals. To a major extent, this phenomenon can be attributed to the rise of the Palestine Liberation Organization (PLO) in the 1960s and the growing prominence of Yasser Arafat, and the rise of Nasser and Nasserism amid the Suez Canal crisis in 1956, both promoting the Arab Nationalist ideology. As the Israeli army defeated Egyptian and Jordanian troops in 1967 who earlier had control over the Gaza Strip and West Bank respectively, in 1967 the idea of Arab unity faced a large setback and the Palestinian question became the priority as the key conflict impeding the dream of Arab unity. Nevertheless, this development granted Palestinians a chance for unity and self-determination as a sovereign state or at least in favor of autonomy, since the territo-

ries were no more torn apart by different authorities (Ashrawi, 1978:77-78). The decade was also characterized by the rise of Rakah, the first political party organized by the Palestinians living within the Israeli borders, a party that won Palestinians recognition throughout the Arab world, as Ashrawi (1978) points out in her essay.

The late 1960s and early to mid 1970s were generally characterized by widespread revolutionary struggle which manifested itself in a series of uprisings in 1973-76 (Ashrawi, 77). Edward Said delineates this period in Palestinian history as characterized by "daring frankness, an unusual new cosmopolitanism in which figures such as Fanon, Mao and Guevara entered the Arab political idiom, and the audacity (perhaps even brashness) attendant upon a political movement proposing itself as capable of doing better than many of its benefactors and patrons" (1991:6). This passage prompts an important characteristic of both Black Art and the Palestinian Culture of Resistance. Fanon, Guevara and Mao were just as relevant for construction of the Palestinian political orientation as the African American one. Fanon was one of the original Black thinkers to emphasize the connection between Arab and African colonial oppression. The author of the idea of the rise of the "consciousness of the colonized," he was also one of the scholars teaching the crucial role of culture for the anti-oppression struggles. Mao was not only a legendary Communist leader but also a poet and an historical figure whom Baraka actively embraced in the process of his political growth, in turn embraced by Kanafani and many other Palestinian Marxist and Communist thinkers. Guevara was one of the first figures connecting the history of African American and Latin American revolutionaries. Guevara also became a symbol of revolutionary communist ideals adopted by the Popular Front of Liberation of Palestine—Kanafani, for example, belonged to the Communist Party. The Communist and

Socialist nature of Palestinian nationalist ideology was also one of the major ideological forces that inspired the nationalist thinking of the African-American community. James Smethurst, the author of *The Black Arts Movement,* points out that it was the Communist Party of the United States of America that first declared the need for an independent republic for African Americans, due to racial and class segregation and injustice imposed upon the people. Larry Neal, another prominent figure in the history of Black Arts movement, in his famous essay with the identical title, defined the movement as an "aesthetic and spiritual sister of Black Power movement."

Harlow's essay mentioned earlier reveals the connection between the armed and artistic struggles. Quoting Kanafani, she writes: "extreme importance of the cultural form of resistance is no less valuable than armed resistance" (1986:10). Henceforth, the relationship between Black Art and Black Power movements was similar to the one between the Palestinian Culture of Resistance and the armed anti-occupation struggle.

Like the aforementioned political movements, these cultural counterparts were parts of a much larger Third World liberation struggle. Barbara Harlow further writes about the significance of the Third World context in Kanafani's work: "Ghassan Kanafani, referring to Palestinian literature as resistance literature, is writing within a historical context, a context which may immediately be situated in the contemporary liberation struggles against Western imperialist domination of Africa, South America, the Middle and the Far East" (Harlow,10). The global nature of artistic liberation struggles was also an extremely important aspect of the Black Arts Movement, as Larry Neal points out in "Any Day Now": "The Black Arts movement…reasons that this linking must take place along lines that are rooted in an Afro-American and Third World historical and cultural sensibility. By 'Third

World,' we mean that we see our struggle in the context of the global confrontations occurring in Africa, Asia, and Latin America. We identify with all of the righteous forces in those places which are struggling for human dignity" (1972:149). The significance of the Third World movement was inevitable, taking into account the homogeneous nature of the historical roots of the Black Arts Movement and the Palestinian Culture of Resistance. Both movements emerged as a result of political self-awareness and self-education conducted by people struggling for a nationalist cause, and both were under the powerful influence of Pan-Arab and Pan-African thought. It is important to note that just as the Palestinian cause became a symbol of Arab Nationalist-struggle, African nationalist moods adopted by Black Americans brought about the rebirth of African nationalist ideas.

These two ideologies of resistance refer to similar tendencies of ideologies of oppression faced by African Americans and Palestinians alike. In his most controversial book, *The Question of Palestine*, Edward Said dedicates a great deal of attention to the similarities embedded in imperialist Western and Zionist thought. Said emphasizes the idea of the "pioneering spirit" of American as well as Israeli immigrants as the major ideological cause of unconditional support of the Zionist project by the United States government. Said draws an even clearer parallel between the Palestinian and African American experience in his article "Reflections on Twenty years of Palestinian History." The author reveals the horrific conditions Palestinian workers faced while working in newly created State of Israel. Even though, unlike African slaves, Palestinians were paid for their work, those were less than minimum wages; workers were exploited almost to death and did not have any rights, despite their inhuman toil. Said describes terrible practices of Israeli employers, revealing that the workers who could not return home and had to spend the night were not given any freedom within Green Line (Israeli borders) and were sometimes buried alive when locked at the dark rooms for the night. The author notes a shocking detail of Palestinian history as he points out that these workers often identified themselves as "slaves." This inhuman treatment is not only an echo of the terrifying practices of the slave owners during the antebellum era in the United Sates, but also is reminiscent of the great turmoil and painful irony of African American history: just as in the case of the Palestinian "slave," it was the Black slave, displaced from the native land, who built the ground for United Sates the way Palestinian slaves built Israel's prosperous capitalist system. Both African Americans and Palestinians were not only stripped of nationhood but were also forced into building the wellbeing of their oppressor. Said draws more and more parallels between Palestinian and African-American history as he deepens his analysis of the Palestinian experience: "the entire tenor of Zionist and Western discourse about the Palestinians has been to reduce us to so problematic, eccentric, and unthinkable a level as to make our every effort to appear to be human only a confirmation of our dehumanized, permanently subaltern status" (Said, 1979:31). Said notices another aspect of Zionist ideology that is painfully reminiscent of the racist ideology of the United States towards African Americans, pointed out by W.E.B. Du Bois in his 1903 *The Souls of Black Folk*, when he asks his famous question "how does it feel to be a problem?" "Demographical problem" is the way that Zionist thinkers described Palestinian population long before the creation of Israel. This locution is still used by extremist Zionists.

Arabs in Israel or Arab-Israelis, who remained on their land after the partition was executed in 1948 and the 1967 exodus, became second class citizens in the country and faced multiple levels of economic, social, and political segregation. Even having obtained some political power in the Knesset, the status of Arab Israelis still resembles the African-American one. The famous Zionist motto "Land without people to people without land," as pointed out by Said in *The Question of Palestine,* is the best possible example of the dehumanizing nature of the Zionist attitude towards Palestinians. The concept is also reflected in the terrible portrayals of Black Americans that allowed dehumanizing practices to take place during antebellum and later Jim Crow eras.

III. AFRICAN AMERICAN SUPPORT FOR THE CAUSE OF PALESTINE

Given their own history of oppression by the West, it is not surprising that African Americans were one of the earliest communities to express solidarity with the Palestinian cause. Many members of the Black Arts Movement and African American thinkers in general instantly recognized the neo-colonial nature of the state of Israel, while almost the entire world community was still viewing Jewish people and Israelis solely as victims. African-Americans openly protested against its creation. As early as 1968, Larry Neal wrote: "The Negro leadership voiced strong support of the Israelis during the conflict and they were given a great deal of exposure in the racist press. But the nationalists had no adequate means of presenting the Arab side of the conflict. So powerful was the pro-Israeli propaganda that most pro-Arab militants were labeled as racist 'anti-Semites.' Popular approval of Zionist aspirations in the Middle East is not based on Biblical mysticism, but on the cumulative results of good propaganda for over forty years. An analysis of international realities clearly indicates that Zionist interests are decidedly pro-Western and that these interests are neo-colonialist in nature and design" (1968:143).

This rare example of support for the Palestinian cause at such early stage is not the only instance of the African-American community openly proclaiming sympathy with the Palestinian community. In fact, the Black Arts Movement contained the largest number of African Americans declaring the right for a Palestinian sovereignty and the racist and neo-colonial nature of the Zionist discourse. In 1970, the founding convention of the Congress of African People (CAP), one of the most important Black Power organizations, was held in Atlanta, Georgia. The congress gathered a great number of important black political figures from all over the country and beyond its borders including the ambassador of Guinea, Louis Farrakhan of the Nation of Islam, Imari Obadale from the Republic of New Africa, African Liberation Army spokesmen, Jesse Jackson, and many others. The Congress was a brilliant example of African-American unity and readiness for sovereignty. The congress produced a great number of documents touching upon technological, social, educational, religious and artistic issues essential for the creation of an independent republic, and made a clear affirmation of their ideological and political standpoint (Baraka 1970: 7-10). Howard Fuller, the president of Malcolm X Liberation University in North Carolina, expressed a radical and complete support of the Palestinian cause and directly compared the history of the creation of Israel and the United States: "Israel is a settler colony. There is no such place as Israel. It is Palestine, and so that all of you, all of you niggers who saw fit to sign that document saying that you support Israel, you are supporting nothing. We must understand that those Europeans, who call themselves Jews moved to Palestine, took the land in 1948. This is what it's all about, and America is a settler colony. So that while we're dealing on that level, then we will understand that we are Africans, Europeans are Europeans, not Americans, not Israeleans, not Afrikaners, they are Europeans, and it is these people that we must address ourselves to" (Baraka,1970: 59). It is impossible to talk about the history of African-American and Pales-

tinian relations without mentioning the African American man who was one of the designers of the Partition Plan and supporters of the idea of a "Jewish Homeland" in Palestine. Ralph Bunche, a prominent scholar, civil rights activist, prominent NAACP member, the first African American honored with a Noble Prize for Peace in 1949 and one of the key designers of the UN Declaration of Human rights, was in fact the first public figure in United States to support the Palestinian cause (Mann, 166). Peggy Mann describes his journey to Palestine as a part of a United Nations Special Committee on Palestine. Mann describes the complexity of the research process and the prolonged hesitation of Bunche, who while in Jerusalem realized the historical importance of Palestine for the three major monotheistic religions. And even though he chose to support the decision to create Israel, he was one of the very few to realize the catastrophic effects of this decision for the Palestinians. As early as 1951, Bunche gave a speech at the National War College in Washington, declaring the solidarity with the Palestinian people: "The real victims of this whole conflict—and they have been successfully at each stage more victimized—have been the Arabs of Palestine" (Bunche, 1970). Bunche was one of the very few who could see beyond the discourse victimizing the Jewish European population, and even though he recognized the horror of the Holocaust and sympathized with the Jewish cause, he did not fail to see the unjust and imperial nature of the creation of the Jewish Homeland in Palestine.

IV. THE ROLE OF CULTURE AND THE ARTS IN THE TWO LIBERATORY MOVEMENTS

The history of prolonged trauma shared by African Americans and Palestinians finds its traces in the Black Arts Movement and the Palestinian Culture of Resistance. The dehumanizing practices and, even more significantly *ideas,* found in Zionism and the racist ideologies of the United States became the target of African American and Palestinian revolutionary artists. Fanon wrote in *The Wretched of the Earth* (1968) that to destroy a culture means to destroy its people. Said dedicated a large portion of his work *Culture and Imperialism* (1994) to the discourse between culture and empire. Both Palestinian and African-American experiences are illuminating examples of the fact that culture is one of the main targets of the oppressors. African Americans were stripped of their language, religion, and traditions, Palestinians were denied any manifestations of their national identity under Jordanian and Egyptian rule which became even harsher and all-penetrating as the West Bank, and Gaza strip came under Israeli control. Hanan Ashrawi, a Palestinian woman, activist, poet, and scholar, provides a detailed description of cultural oppression in her "The Contemporary Palestinian Poetry of Occupation" (1978). She reveals the strong literary surveillance and forbidden nationalist symbols, censoring even the colors of the Palestinian flag. Arabs in Israel did not escape that fate as well, and unfortunately a portion of them lost a great deal of their cultural connections with Palestine.

Malcolm X realized the importance of culture for African American nationhood at a very early stage, encouraging his fellow African Americans to get rid of the "religion of the white devil" and embrace Islam. X is also one of the first African American leaders to criticize the creation of the state of Israel and the neo-colonial nature of this project. The artists who dedicated themselves and their work to the creation and burgeoning of the Black Arts movement saw culture and art as an essential aspect of their nationalist struggle. Larry Neal wrote in the essay titled "Any Day Now: Black Art and Black Liberation": "The Black Arts movement preaches that liberation is inextricably bound up with politics and culture.

The culture gives us a revolutionary moral vision and a system of values and a methodology around which to shape the political movement. When we say 'culture,' we do not merely mean artistic forms. We mean, instead, the values, the life styles, and the feelings of the people as expressed in everyday life. The total liberation of Blues People cannot be affected if we do not have a value system, a point of reference, a way of understanding what we see and hear every day around us. If we do not have a value system that is, in reality, more moral than the oppressor's, then we cannot hope to change society" (1972:159). Culture similarly presents a major source of national identity for Palestinians and African-Americans alike. Ashrawi (1978) reveals the profound significance of culture for Palestinian nationalism when she notices that while independence was still a dream in the political realm it constituted reality in the cultural sense. The independent Palestinian state and a sovereign African-American republic gained cultural presence before the actual political realization, drawing the actual borders of these states by means of cultural expression.

V. THE SPECIFIC ROLE OF POETRY

Culture is an extremely complex concept comprising a great scope of artistic and ideological constituents; my specific area of concentration for this article is poetry. This choice is indicated by the cultural traditions of both groups of people, as well as the political and artistic characteristics of the Black Arts Movement and the Palestinian Culture of Resistance. Poetry is the most ancient genre of Arab artistic tradition, and goes back to the century-long experiments with linguistic and poetic forms that fascinate and still inspire the modern and postmodern Arab poets. Legends are told about blind Palestinian poets at the refugee camps in Lebanon, uneducated and sometimes even illiterate, who compose verses of amazing poetic skill that keep the tradition alive. Abdelwahab Elmessiri, a distinguished Egyptian scholar and professor of English, writes about the unifying power of poetry that kept Palestinian poets inside Israel connected with their fellow poets beyond the borders and checkpoints: "Palestinian poets, even as they were being harassed and at times terrorized in Israel, even as they were experiencing the pains of exile outside their homeland, still participated in a living historical process that helped them maintain a sense of belonging, thereby overcoming the deep sense of alienation resulting from dislocation, dispersion, and oppression" (1981:78). Further in his argument, Elmessiri provides an overt explanation of this phenomenon, revealing that Palestinian resistance chose poetry over any other artistic mode due to its great history that became a way of asserting its Arab identity (79). The artists of the Black Arts Movement who were also striving for the resurrection of African tradition chose poetry with the exactly same motif, for oral tradition is also considered a major genre of African cultural tradition.

Oral as opposed to written nature of African and Arab poetry is not the only aspect of those poetic traditions that manifests itself in Palestinian and African-American nationalist poetry of the 1960s and 1970s. In "The Palestinian Wedding" (1981) Elmessiri points out the way Palestinian poets would allude to mythology and especially heroic epics of Arab poetic and oral tradition in order to awaken a sense of national pride and a sense of dignity after long years of subjugation and dehumanization. These figures include great poets such as Al-Mutanabi and Antar (79). Antar is a son of African woman and a rich Arab man. Born as a slave, Antar wins his freedom and a high social status after demonstrating his might and noble qualities as a warrior and a distinguished poet whose character is reminiscent of the ideals of African American and Palestinian national struggles in the '60s and '70s. Another common mythological reference

found in African-American and Palestinian nationalist poetry is the allusions to Egyptian mythology, specifically the gods Osiris and Isis, which is widely used by Ishmael Reed and Darwish, and many other African American and Palestinian poets of that period.

At its founding convention, Congress of African Peoples held a special session on creativity and art emphasizing its crucial importance for the creation of an independent African republic in the United States. Much discussion there was dedicated to poetry, its prophetic and changing powers, its uniqueness and features distinguishing it from the Western poetic tradition (mainly its strong connection with the oral tradition) and its importance for affirming of the African identity. As a result a set of resolutions were made granting unconditional support of the poetry editions such as *Cricket, Journal of Black Poetry* and encouraging the creation of newer and newer ones (Baraka, 1970:215). As Smethurst points in *Black Arts Movement*, the importance of poetry for the nationalist struggle of African Americans did not need any introduction or reassurance as Amiri Baraka ended the conference with a poem as opposed to a conventional conclusive political speech. The poem titled "It's Nation Time" provided a quintessence of the Pan African and revolutionary nationalist ideas, reaffirming the significance of ideology and even metaphysical nature of their revolutionary struggle and once again revealing the global nature of the change that they are seeking:

Time to
get
together
time to be one strong fast energy space
...
black genius rise in spirit muscle
...
the black man is the future of the world
...
come out niggers

all niggers negroes must change up
come together in unity unify
for nation time
it's nation time (Baraka,1970:101).

"It's Nation Time" becomes the motto of the Conference and reaffirms the overwhelming spirit of unity and readiness for political self-determination.

Palestinian poetry is also characterized by a prolonged political history. Mahmoud Darwish is known for editing a great number of political documents produced by the PLO. The trace the poetry left on the political documents of the Palestinian Liberation movement is profound. Olivier Carre, a French scholar specializing in the Middle East, dedicated his research to the analysis of conceptual combinations in selected political documents issued by the PLO and a structural analysis of Mahmoud Darwish's poetry. He attributes his motivation to a great number of historical peculiarities of the African-American struggles and those of the Palestinian community within the state of Israel, the Occupied Territories and the global Palestinian Diaspora. Even a brief review of Palestinian history of the 1960s and 1970s will reveal that all the key political figures such as Darwish, Kanafani, Zayyad, Jubran, Ashrawi and many others are also the most prominent and the most influential poets in the history of the Palestinian Literature. A similar tendency is found in the history of the Black Arts Movement when poets such as Neal, Baraka, and Sanchez were active participants in the political life of the African-American community. Nikki Giovanni describes the dangers involved in her revolutionary political and poetic activity in "My Poem":

my phone is tapped
my mail is opened
they've caused me to turn
on all my old friends
and all my new lovers (2003:86).

Exile and imprisonment are also an integral part of many Palestinian poet activists such as Darwish, Mutawakkil Taha, and many others. Poetry was now not a purely artistic expression, but often a major political crime. The Black Arts Movement and the Palestinian culture of Resistance became movements to erase the borders between poetry and politics. Their revolutionary aesthetics forever transformed Palestinian and African-American poetry.

The key members of the Black Arts Movement had a clear set of standards for what poetry ought to be and ought to do. Maulana Karenga, an African-American theorist and activist, clearly identifies requirements and functions of African American poetry: "Art must be functional, collective, and committed. Collective: done by Black people, about Black people and for Black people. Black art must expose the enemy, praise the people and support the revolution" (Baker,9). In her essay "Palestinian Poetry of Occupation," Ashrawi points out the need to address "simple people" in order to become an "effective instrument of resistance" as realized by Palestinian poets and described by Mahmoud Darwish in "Concerning Poetry":

A poet
says
If my poems please my friends
And anger my enemies
Then I'm a poet.
and I shall speak! (Ahsrawi, 1978:87).

Further on, Ashrawi clearly defines the role of poetry through the role of the Palestinian poets: "…They are national figures, symbols of resistance and political as well as aesthetic consciousness, who are wielding their mighty pens in the face of the enemy" (1978:82-83). Such an overt lauding of the resistance poets is contrasted with the poets whose art is detached from the community and the political struggle. Ashrawi points out that their art finds its inspiration in the Western tradition and not in the ancient Arab poetic realm, and she appears overtly critical of this kind of poetry, describing it as abstract and "incomprehensible" (84)

The figure of a poet inevitably undergoes a great transformation as a result of these new aesthetic dmands during the 1960s. Etheridge Knight describes the mission of the African American poet in "Black Poets Who Think of Suicide":

For Black Poets belong to Black people. Are
the flutes of Black Lovers. Are
Organs of Black Sorrows. Are
The Trumpets of Black Warriors.
    (Knight,52)

He reveals the essential importance of the poet, and that more than any artist during any other historical period the poet unconditionally and completely belongs to his/her community and to the revolutionary nationalist cause. African American as well as Palestinian poets gain a status of tremendous importance, they are dignified and praised, raised to a prophetic, almost divine status and are simultaneously an integral part of their community. Ahmad Dahbour speaks about his mission as a poet with a true poetic beauty:

I'll do it. I'll tell the trees to unite
I'll tell the sorrows to join forces
I'll tell the motherland to unite
And I promise
To do likewise
…From here, the new begins, and
childhood shall return to
Laila's womb, be born in the camp, and the
camp, and the camp shall grow
And grow, then it will run
In the direction of the water spring and
engender a world
And I shall have time to write a different
poem (1992:141).

Dahbour places himself as a spiritual

leader, calling for unity and simultaneously identifying himself with the people in his promise "to do likewise." He also affirms his devotion to the revolutionary struggle, saying that he will not write of anything else until the victory is achieved. As poets are transformed into politicians and, more significantly, active fighters in the national struggle, it is not shocking to anyone that the traditionally lofty and fragile poem obtains a firm iron form and turns into a weapon. Rashid Husain recognizes the horrors of the occupation, and even though he appears to regret the new militant function of his poetry, he affirms its inevitability:

Against a child becoming a hero at ten

Against a tree heart sprouting mines

Against my orchard's branches becoming
    gallows

Against erecting scaffolds among the roses
    of my land

Against what you will—

But after my country, my comrades, and
    my youth were burnt,

How can my poems not turn into guns?
    (1992:174-175)

Amiri Baraka's "Black Art," anthem of the movement, describes the transformation poetry underwent as a result of the Black Arts Movement. Poems are also compared to weapons, torn away from tidy white pages and sent right into the crowded streets; poems are no longer metaphysical but material, active participants—moreover, "The Right Arm of the Revolution":

Poems are bullshit unless they are
Teeth or trees or lemons piled
On a step…
Fuck poems

And they are useful, they shoot
Come at you, love what you are,
Breathe like wrestlers…
We want live
Wards of the hip world live flesh &
Coursing blood. Hearts Brains
Souls splintering fire. We want poems
Like fists beating niggers out of Jocks
Or dagger poems
…
We want "poems that kill."
Assassin poems, Poems that shoot
Guns. Poems that wrestle cops into alleys
And take their weapons leaving them
        dead…
Knockoff
Poems for dope selling wops or slick half-
        white
Politicians Airplane poems.
…setting fire and death to
whities ass…
Poem scream poison gas on beasts in green
        berets
Clean out the world for virtue and love,
Let there be no love poems written
Until love can exist freely and
Cleanly…
We want a black poem. And a
Black World.
Let the world be a Black Poem
And let All Black People Speak This Poem
        Silently
Or LOUD (Baraka, 1968:302-303).

The poem is a quintessence of the Black
Arts Movement aesthetics. It reflects their
transformation of aesthetic form and func-
tions, erasing the traditional connotation of
poetry as a metaphysical concept. The poets
of Palestinian Resistance and the Black Arts
Movement breathe life into poetry. A poem
is beautiful not only if it rouses us into an
aesthetic frenzy, but also if it can empathize
with people's pain, encourage and support
the people, be a helping hand, and a Molo-
tov cocktail when needed. A poem does not
belong on a tidy page of a book, but on dirty
walls of ghettos and refugee camps. A poem

is not only heard during a reading, a poem
is shouted at the demonstration to shatter
the oppressor. A poem cries with a wid-
owed woman and marches alongside the
guerrilla fighters on a victory day. A poem
was an anthem for the dream land that Afri-
can Americans and Palestinians were striv-
ing for in the 1960s and 1970s.

In order to achieve this goal, it is not
enough to transform the essence of poetry,
and give it a new life. It is also essential to
turn poetry into a movement, a public prop-
erty. Poetry readings broke out of the walls
of theaters into the streets and started to be
heard all over the country, especially in
Denver, New Orleans, Chicago, and Har-
lem. Street performances, plays, debates, a
whole street culture sprung out as a major
artistic and political phenomenon in the his-
tory of the United States. Palestinians were
denied such means of artistic expression,
but even under strong Israeli surveillance
they managed to organize an entire under-
ground movement, gathering large groups
of people all around the occupied territories
for poetry reading sessions, panel discus-
sions, seminars and lectures with Birzeit
University as their main setting. The Black
Arts Movement, like the Palestinian Culture
of Resistance, proved their intention of cre-
ating art "for the simple people" in every
way possible, to spread the message of free-
dom while often risking their own.

The new connotations, functions, and
profound political influences brought about
a number not only of thematic but also sty-
listic characteristics to the African American
and Palestinian poetic tradition alike. The
functions of resistance poetry, as described
earlier by Karenga, meant that poetry repre-
sents the entire African American commu-
nity, with all the cultural peculiarities that
distinguish it from the rest of American so-
ciety. The essential aspect of these features is
of course the linguistic tradition of African
Americans. Instances of this tendency are
found in every single piece of poetry written
during the Black Arts Movement. The poets

no longer see the vernacular criticized by both African-Americans and the rest of the population as a sign of ignorance or illiteracy; the poets embrace it as their own language as it becomes a significant tool in creating a distinct national culture. Other poets such as Ahmed Leghraham Alhamisi would not only write using the African American vernacular but also use African languages seeking connection to their linguistic tradition, like in his poem titled UHURU.

Another prominent figure of the Black Arts Movement, Marvin X, sees Arabic language and Islamic culture as essential aspects of African cultural heritage that are lost among the dominant Western traditions. The poet seeks to deconstruct the racist dialectic through reminding the reader of the African origin of human civilization, evoking pride in African ancestry and the color of the skin that has been turned into a stigma through the racism ideologies of the West. The poet calls for reunification of ancient African culture with Arabic language as its vital component. Only when this heritage is resurrected can the ideals of the revolution be achieved:uhuru (freedom.now.swahili.east african lango)

MUSIKmusikMMMUUUsikMUSIK-
    MUSIK
MUSIKMUSIKmusikmusikmusikMUSIK-
    musikkk
You have taken up
the ole folks burden.sent
forth a stronger breed POWpow.powpow-
    pow. crackcrack
    crack.CRASHCRASH.
BOOM.BOOMBOOMBOOMBOOM-
    BOOM.tearing down
The Master's need. With buildings of BLK
    minds.the east
African language
Hujambo Bwana Nigger.Binti
Nigger.Bibi Nigger.YALL NIGGERS
(go forth baby.&let yr beauty
Shine. &shine & shine (1968:424-425).

Al Asl Suddi
The Origin of Blackness
SUDAN La al lawn
Black is not color
Lon kuli min Sudan
ALL colors come from Black
Sudan al harakat
Black is the rhythm.
Al marna tambura
Anata
Ancient
Assi
Primitive
Al awwal sudan kalam
The first word was Black.
Al awwal rajuli sudan
The first man was Black.
Allah sudan
God is Black.
Sudan ilmi akhi
Black knows its brother
Anta mufail mashay min sudan
You can't run from Black.
Anta mufail ghaybay min sudan
You can't hide from Black.
Ka umma sudan
Your mother is Black.
Ka abu sudan
Your father is Black
Ka burka sudan
Your shadow is Black.
Al atun ra'a wa sami sudan
The things you see and hear are Black.
Al atun mufail ra'a wa sami sudan
The things you can't see and hear are Black.
Sudan al asil
Black is reality.
Wahabi, hurriya, adil, masawati
Unity, freedom, justice, equality (1967:33).

Palestinian Resistance Poetry was also written with a deep sense of Arab identity and Arab history. Abdelwahab Elmessiri reveals the richness of images from ancient Arab history in Darwish's "A Lover from Palestine":

I have seen Byzantium's horses
Even though the battle be different.
Beware, oh beware
The lightning struck by my song in the
    granite.
I am the flower of youth and the knight of
    knights!
I am the smasher of Idols.
I plant the Levantine borders
With poems that set eagles free. (1981:79).

Anyone familiarized with ancient Arab history will recognize the figures of poet-activists such as 'Antar (525-619), al-Muttanabi (915-965) and al-Barudi (1840-1904). Along with the profound sense of connection to the histories of their ancestors that the Black Arts Movement poetry and the Palestinian Poetry of Resistance have in common, Palestinian poetry is also characterized with the wide usage of vernacular as opposed to the Classical Arabic language, the language of the Holy Quran. Ya'qoub Hijazi manifests his determination to dedicate his art to the masses, as Ashrawi points out in "The Other Face":

Because I write poems for the human being,
Peasant, oppressed, worker
My letters shall always be known,
Cross the bridge of my tragedy to the more
    beautiful
Write a story…
So that my people may rise to the better
    (88).

The common use of the Black dialect can also be justified by the attempt to distinguish their experience and poetic creation from those of contemporary Arab poets. Examples of the overt support of the Palestinian cause by the African-American community are not limited to open political statements of support, but also are found in examples of artistic cooperation between the artists of the Black Arts Movement and the Palestinian Culture of Resistance. In 1968 Askia Toure, a guest editor of *The*

Journal of Black Poetry, included works by the key figures of the movement in an issue: Salim Joubran, Samih el-Qassem, Tawfiq Zayyad and Mahmoud Darwish. Journal identifies the poets as "poet, guerrilla fighter of occupied Palestine." This gesture, an extremely important aspect of the cultural and political history of both nations, unknown by very few, once again reaffirms the fact that the two nationalist movements have strong connections, silenced by popular history and in strong need of research and revival for the sake of both of these liberation and anti-racist struggles.

VI. CONCLUSION

The history of the Black Arts Movement and the Palestinian Culture of Resistance do not only resemble and intertwined with each other, they are both a part of the same struggle for independence and self-determination that emerged in the 1960s. The movements are born out of the same historical circumstances and nourished by the same ideals and hopes. They emerge and consciously see themselves as a part of the Third World revolutionary movement, aiming to unify all the oppressed nations in their struggle for independence and equality. The Black Arts Movement and the Palestinian Culture of Resistance seek a sense of belonging and connection to the cultures of their ancestors, which prove to have similar historical and therefore aesthetic traditions. Their struggles are global and all-inclusive, reaching out to all who seek justice, stand out and speak out against dehumanization, strive for the liberation of not only occupied lands but also occupied minds. Palestinian and African American poetry manages to create a powerful sense of unity with the help of the beauty and wisdom of their ancestors.

By using their own cultural forms and language, African-American and Palestinian poets manage to create physical spaces that are unreachable for the enemy and to embody their nationalist dreams not only metaphysically, often transcending this realm and fulfilling the dreams of sovereignty for as long as a poem would last, keeping the dream of independence alive. The movements gained the best from their aesthetic roots and combined them with new revolutionary innovative forms that affirm and fascinate with their poetic skill, originality, and enormous scope of potential and revolutionary energy. Moreover, The Black Arts Movement is the first major example of a strong and open cultural and political support for the Palestinian cause in the history of the United States. Even though it is silenced and seemingly unknown it is a great starting point for the revival for the Palestinian/African-American cultural and political relations.

Despite the enormous scope of political legacy traced in these movements, its most significant achievement does not lie in the ability to transform a poem into a political document, not even into a revolutionary figure, but to mix poetic beauty with passion and hope and transform it into a country.

Works Cited

Alhamisi, Ahmad Legraham. "Uhuru." *Black Fire: An Anthology of Afro-American Writing.* Edited by Amiri Baraka/LeRoi Jones and Larry Neal. New York: Morrow, 1968, 424-427.

Ashrawi, Hanan Mikhail. "The Contemporary Palestinian Poetry of Occupation." *Journal of Palestine Studies.* University of California Press, 1978, 77-101.

Baraka, Imamu Amiri. "Black Art." *Black Fire: an Anthology of Afro-American Writing.* Edited by Amiri Baraka/LeRoi Jones and Larry Neal. New York: Morrow, 1968, 302.

Baraka, Imamu Amiri. "It's Nation Time." *Congress of African Peoples (1970: Atlanta) African Congress: A Documentary of the First Modern Pan-African Congress.* Edited by Imamu Amiri Baraka (LeRoi Jones).

Bunche, Ralph. *Ralph J. Bunche: Selected Speeches and Writing.* Edited by Charles P. Henry. Ann Arbor: University of Michigan Press, 1995.

Congress of African Peoples. *Congress of African Peoples (1970: Atlanta) African Congress; a Documentary of the first Modern pan-African congress.* Edited by Imamu Amiri Baraka (LeRoi Jones).

Dahbour, Ahmad. "I Do Not Renounce Madness." *Anthology of Modern Palestinian Literature.* Edited by Salma Khadra Jayyusi. New York:

Columbia University Press, 1992.

Darwish, Mahmoud. "We Travel Like all Other People. *Unfortunately it was Paradise: Selected Poems by Mahmoud Darwish.* Edited by Munir Akash and Carolyn Forché, Sinan Antoon and Amira El Zein. Berkeley: University of California Press, 2003, 10.

Darwish, Mahmoud. "A Lover From Palestine." Elmessiri, Amdelwahab E. "The Palestinian Wedding: Major Themes of Contemporary Palestinian Resistance Poetry." *Journal of Palestine Studies.* University of California Press, 1981, 77-99.

Darwish, Mahmoud. "Concerning Poetry." Ashrawi, Hanan Mikhail. "The Contemporary Palestinian Poetry of Occupation." *Journal of Palestine Studies.* University of California Press, 1978. 77-101.

Elmessiri, Amdelwahab E. "The Palestinian Wedding: Major Themes of Contemporary Palestinian Resistance Poetry." *Journal of Palestine Studies.* University of California Press, 1981, 77-99.

Giovanni, Nikki. *The Collected Poetry of Nikki Giovanni 1968-1998.* New York: William Morrow, 2003.

Harlow, Barbara. "Return to Haifa: 'Opening the Borders' in Palestinian Literature." *Social Text.* Duke University Press, 1986, 3-23.

Husain, Rashid. "Against." *Anthology of Modern Palestinian Literature.* Edited by Salma Khadra Jayyusi. New York: Columbia Univeristy Press, 1992.

Hijazi, Ya'cob. "The Other face." Ashrawi, Hanan Mikhail. "The Contemporary Palestinian Poetry of Occupation." *Journal of Palestine Studies.* University of California Press, 1978.

Mann, Peggy. *Ralph Bunche, UN peacemaker.* New York: Coward, McCann & Geoghegan, 1975.

Knight, Etheridge. "For Black Poets Who Think of Suicide." *The Essential Etheridge Knight.* Pittsburgh: University of Pittsburgh Press, 1986.

Neal, Larry. "Any Day Now: Black Art and Black Liberation." *Black Poets and Prophets; The Theory, Practice, and Esthetics of the Pan-Africanist Revolution.* Eds. Woodie King and Earl Anthony, NY: New American Library, 1972, 148-65.

Neal, Larry. "Black Power in the International Context." *The Black Power Revolt.* Barbour and Floyd B., Boston: Porter Sargent, 1968, 136-46.

Neal, Larry. "The Black Arts Movement" *The Drama* The MIT Press, 1968, 29-39.

Said, Edward W. "Intifada and Independence." *Social Text.* Duke University Press, 1989, 23-39.

Said, Edward W. "Reflections on Twenty Years of Palestinian History." *Journal of Palestine Studies.* University of California Press, 1991, 5-22.

X, Marvin. "Al asl suddi." *Journal of Black Poetry.* Edited by Joe Goncalves. San Francisco, 1967, 33.

Works Consulted

Fanon, Frantz. *The Wretched of the Earth.* New York: Grove Press.1968

Said, Edward W. *Culture and Imperialism.* New York: Vintage Books, 1994.

Said, Edward W. *The Question of Palestine.* New York: Times Books, 1979.

Smethurst, James Edward. *The Black Arts Movement: literary nationalism in the 1960s and 1970s.* Chapel Hill: University of North Carolina Press, 2005.

Darwish's Essentialist Poetics in a State of Siege

Patrick Sylvain

Brown University, Harvard University, and University of Massachusetts Boston

———————————————

sylvainpa@att.net

Abstract: This article analyzes Darwish's creative dissidence and proposes a literary anthropological mapping that exposes his own relative historicity—his truth about Israel's occupation on the one hand, and his love for life and for his native land as a quintessentially locative human condition on the other. The existential echo that reverberates through Darwish's language is a calling, a desire for home—home in the poetic corpus and home for the nation. Socio-critical analysis of Mahmoud Darwish's poetics about his homeland requires that the corpus of his works be treated almost as a literary anthropological philosophy by relativizing it within the homo-historical and social literary contexts in which it was produced. My assessment of assigned categories onto Darwish's poetic corpus is an interpretive ontological signifying in order to map his literary evolution as it pertains to the identified categories (1-Formative, 2-Sublime, 3-Global). This assessment is not presumptuous or exhaustive; it is a theoretical study that tries to situate Darwish's poetic discourse within a socio-historical field and beyond the mere literary framework—a necessity given the broad scope of his works and philosophy.

I. INTRODUCTION

The intersection of violence, national identity and literature has always been one of my intellectual interests, as has the plight and culture of Palestinians. The latter is due largely to the significant number of Palestinians that have migrated to my native Haiti since the first *Intifada* in 1987, and also because of the loss of a dear Haitian-Palestinian elder, Antoine Izmery, to political violence in October 1994. Additionally, my relationships with Palestinian writers such as Suheir Hammad and Ibtisam Barrakat have solidified my understanding of Palestinian literary traditions, and have led me to find a deep appreciation for Palestinian Mahmoud Darwish's work.

This essay is not about Palestinian history nor is it a comparative study of Palestinian poetry. Rather, it is about a writer who became dissident and exposed in his own relative historicity, his truth about Israel's occupation on the one hand, and his love for life and for his native land as a quintessentially locative human condition, on the other. In 1948, Mahmoud Darwish was six years old when his interrupted childhood brutally confronted exile. Thousands of Palestinians were forced to exile due to the systematic occupation by the Israelis. For Darwish, severance from the

Patrick Sylvain is a Haitian language instructor at Brown University, a language coach at Harvard University, and has also worked as an adjunct professor in anthropology at UMass Boston. A writer, social critic, translator and photographer, he has been published in several anthologies, magazines and reviews including: *African American Review, Agni, American Poetry Anthology, American Poetry Review,* "The Best of Beacon, 1999," "The Butterfly's Way," *Callaloo, Caribbean Writers, Confrontation, Crab Orchard Review, Haitian Times, Human Architecture: Journal of the Sociology of Self-Knowledge, Massachusetts Review, The Oxford Book of Caribbean Verse* (2005), *Ploughshares, Revue Noire* and "Step Into the World." His latest bilingual poetry collection *Love, Lust & Loss* was published by Mémoire d'Encrier (Dec. 2005). He is currently working on a collection of essays entitled: *Poetry as Political Discourse.*

homeland gave birth to his poetry, and commenced a love affair with location and dislocation. Throughout Mahmoud Darwish's poetics is the linkage of individuals or occupied entities to the ideal of a universal struggle for freedom and liberty from oppression, and a link to the "beauty" of life and language through the creative process—thus affirming Wellek & Warren's notion that: "[t]he work of literature is an aesthetic object, capable of arousing aesthetic experience" (1984: 241). And it was Darwish's creative work and precise language that transcended his experience not only as a Palestinian writer, but also as a writer who aroused the universal, while managing the aesthetic transmission of the oppressive side of the human condition under occupation. In his prosaic memoir, *Memory for Forgetfulness*, Darwish writes in hauntingly surrealist manner:

"He's looking for a pair of eyes, for a shared silence or reciprocal talk. He's looking for some kind of participation in this death, for a witness who can give evidence, for a gravestone over a corpse, for the bearer of news about the fall of a horse, for a language of speech and silence, and for less boring wait for certain death. For what this steel and these iron beasts are screaming is that no one will be left in peace, and no one will count our dead" (1995: 24).

What Darwish aroused first in the Palestinians and then in the rest of the world is the aesthetic value of an experience that is free from oppression. He also brought to the surface an aesthetic that spoke truth to power and exposed the experienced madness of occupation. "Poetry is a dangerous game. It sometimes drives people to find a substitute for absence. It happens to me sometimes. At such times, I feel a sense of dangerous repose, that what I have written

has given me respite from inner torment, has liberated me" (Darwish, 1997 Documentary).

It has been established to the point of becoming cliché, that true poets, conscientious poets, are depositories of societal memories as well as witnesses to human conditions. In an essay written between 1944 and 1945, entitled *Poetry and Knowledge*, the young French-Martinican poet, Aimé Césaire, lucidly described the role of the poet. This description easily connects to the essence and the life of Darwish: "the poet is that very ancient yet new being, at once very complex and very simple, who at the limit of dream and reality, of day and night, between absence and presence, searches for and receives in the sudden triggering of inner cataclysms the password of connivance and power" (1990: 1vi). Mahmoud Darwish became the ancient and the new, the social chronicler of Palestinian emotions—emotions felt, or repressed, the whole gamut of human emotions in various states of siege and exile. The notion of the poet as chronicler is further supported by musings of a prominent Syrian critic, Subbi Hadidi, who writes that: "All cultures, like Arabic culture, attributed a special role to their poets at a particular moment of their history. It became incumbent upon poets everywhere to speak for their communities, to find answers to existential questions, to give poetry a power that was national and cultural, spiritual and material, aesthetic and informative" (2008: 97).

The existential echo that reverberates through Darwish's language is a calling, a desire for home—home in the poetic corpus and home for the nation. Through his lived conditions as a "stateless being," Darwish learned and transmitted his "lessons" through verses, his creative freedom-land. According to Fady Joudah, a major translator of Darwish's work into English, "Darwish does not disengage the act of writing from its subject matter. Instead, he performs a twinning. The beloved is not exclusively a woman or a land, self or other, but also poem and prose" (2007: xvi). Perhaps, in a state of siege or exile, the poet has learned that in order to survive or to maintain one's humanity, one must love arduously. Darwish's love is constant throughout his poems; it is as if he is reminding himself and his enemies of love, and the sense of what it could be like to create a bond based on human values rather than religious or capital dogmas, values that transcend constructed borders. In a sense, the social and material constructs engineered by the Israelis to maintain the Palestinian as the other, become their own legacies. Their dehumanization and Darwish's *Earth Poem* clearly elucidates that point:

> And they searched his chest
> But could only find his heart
> And they searched his heart
> But could only find his people
> And they searched his voice
> But could only find his grief
> And they searched his grief
> But could only find his prison
> And they searched his prison
> But could only see themselves in chains
>   (1993: 563)

What pulls me in and through Darwish's monde poetic is his sense of humanity that seems to constantly restore hope and love even when Israeli tanks and aircrafts are pounding Ramallah, Gaza or other occupied territories. His restoration or established desire to love becomes the specific point of humanity that occupation cannot put under control. This desire to love in what seems to be a fragmented "nation" restores a constant hope of a new dawn. This is where lives; despite attempts to confine, imprison, and destroy his home, he continues to strive by what the poet refers to as an intuitive sense of survival, the "sixth sense." In the epic book of poems *A State of Siege* (2002), Darwish's poetic sensibility and journalistic training formed a literary symbiosis that expanded a new vastness of the creative language into a space that heaved surprises and pain:

> The soldiers measure the distance
>   between being
> and nonbeing
> with a tank's scope ...
>
> We measure the distance with our
>   bodies
> and mortar shells... with the sixth
>   sense (2007: 125)

The spatial confinement of the occupied Palestinian territory is defined ideologically and reinforced through a military apparatus where marginalized subjects are further objectified and scoped as if as mechanical objects placed on shooting ranges to be snuffed into infinity. However, the poet is reminding us that the nonbeing-like-object is a conscientious being, a highly developed subject who is able, at times, to measure high-speed mortars "with a sixth sense" because of his experience with habitual Israeli shellings. Darwish's poetics are not allegories of provocation against Israel, but rather, they are historical *mise en abyme*, a form of poetic historical mirroring, a reproduction of the 'is'. Thus, Darwish's dissidence is a result of his accurate reproduction of the "is" that Israel produces. In the bilingual edition of the Arabic poetry anthology *Victims of a Map*, Darwish's selected poems elucidate the problematic of the Israeli occupation by poetically mapping the cartography of emotional and spatial confinement. In the poem "We Fear for a Dream," Darwish's brilliance at aesthetically historicizing through poetic means becomes evident:

> We know you have abandoned us, built
>   for us prisons and called them
> the paradise of oranges.
> We go on dreaming. Oh, desired
>   dream. We steal our days from
>   those

Extolled by our myths.
We fear for you, we're afraid of you. We
    are exposed together, you
Shouldn't believe our wives' patience.
    (1984: 17)

Being a dissident is about exposing the
immoral aspects of institutions; it is about
exposing the contradictions inherent in the
superstructure of power, and revealing
what it is like to be the other and to con-
struct one's own ontology about a group's
felt experiences while deconstructing im-
posed myths of the other. "And when we
write, call upon other writers to write, in the
name of creative freedom, we are doing
nothing more than bringing into focus the
points of light and first efforts scattered by
dissension over an idea founded on this
simple assertion: we want to liberate our-
selves, our countries, and our minds and
live in the modern age with competence
and pride" (Darwish, 1995: 140). What the
Israeli government perceived as Darwish's
dissention is nothing more than his funda-
mental right to supremely love his birth-
place, and to be free from control without
consent. Darwish's perceived dissention be-
came the acclamation of Palestinians with a
lucid voice of conscience. According to John
Mikkail Asfour's biographical notes, "Dar-
wish has been influenced by political and
social changes and liberation movements
throughout the world, on which subject he
is an avid reader. Unlike many poets Dar-
wish may claim to have lived his poetry, for
many a time he has faced imprisonment by
the Israeli authorities for his activities in the
pro-Arab faction of the country's Commu-
nist Party, while living and working as a
journalist in Haifa" (1992: 208).

Socio-critical analysis of Mahmoud
Darwish's poetics about his homeland re-
quires that the corpus of his works be
treated almost as a literary anthropological
philosophy by relativizing it within the
homo-historical and social literary contexts
in which it was produced. "In the Arab and
specifically the Palestinian case, aesthetics
and politics are intertwined for a number of
reasons. One is the ever-present repression
and blockage of life, on every level, by the
Israeli occupation, by the dispossession of
an entire nation, and the sense that we are a
nation of exiles. So, that defines our situa-
tion, to which the writer responds. Another
dynamic is the pressure of the Islamic and
Arabic language tradition itself, which is
very powerful. Language is the central cul-
tural expression of the Arabs" (Said, 2003:
164). With the centrality of language as an
integral part in the expressive modalities of
Mahmoud Darwish's aesthetic project, and
unlike the post-modern writers whose aes-
thetic was to utilize language for language's
sake, Darwish vehicles language with loca-
tive content and referential context.

I discern three informative periods in
the history of his poetics: Formative, or,
what I would classify as Trenchant; Sub-
lime, as Love and Exile; and Global, as Hu-
manity, Return and Dashed Hope.

II. FORMATIVE: THE PERFOLIATION OF TRENCHANT POETICS

My assessment of assigned categories
onto Darwish's poetic corpus is an interpre-
tive ontological signifying in order to map
his literary evolution as it pertains to the
identified categories (1-Formative, 2-Sub-
lime, 3-Global). My assessment is not pre-
sumptuous or exhaustive; it is a theoretical
study that tries to situate Darwish's poetic
discourse within a socio-historical field and
beyond the mere literary framework—a ne-
cessity given the broad scope of his works
and philosophy. In other words, it would
not be at all sufficient to remove the poet
from the social and read his works as simply
as a literary genre, namely poetry, and thus
assign aesthetics, tropes, meters and rhyme
sequences to his work without contemplat-
ing what Chris Miller refers to as "the dissi-
dence of the imagination" (1995: 13).

Darwish's poetic is much more complex than assigned signifiers; hence, I insist upon the use of poetic corpus and discourse as modes of analysis and reference in order to fully grasp his *dissidence of the imagination*, his witnessing.

In 1964, the young Darwish, published a poem entitled "To the Reader" in which he explicitly channeled his politics, and was also conscious of the mode of his expression, namely literati.

> O reader,
> don't expect whispers from me,
> or words of ecstasy:
> this is my suffering!
> A foolish blow in the sand
> and another in the clouds.
> Anger is all I am
> anger, the tinder
> Of fire.
> (1992: 209)

At this, the outset of his formative years, Darwish's poem announced that his noetic consciousness of the needed or expected poetics would be non-pastoral, non-nominal, and non-conventional (made to feel good); but rather, his poetics would be involved in what "is" the actual. Darwish's noesis of the quintessential power of words would later establish him in the realm of poets as understood by Aimé Césaire, one of the most revered poet and statesmen of the postcolonial world. In one of Césaire's essays, 'Poetry and Knowledge' he lucidly affirmed that: "it is not merely with his whole soul, it is with his entire being that the poet approaches the poem. What presides over the poem is not the most lucid intelligence, or the most acute sensibility, but an entire experience: all the women loved, all the desires experienced, all the dreams dreamed, all of the images received or grasped, the whole weight of the body, the whole weight of the mind…" Indeed, it is Darwish's noetic consciousness and experience that informed his poetics, and therein lies the importance of Césaire's assertion of the all-lived experience. "All the possibility[ies]. Around the poem about to be made, the precious vortex: the ego, the id, the world" (1990: xlvii). And in the 1964 poem "To the Reader" Darwish's ego and id were already engaging the world.

In yet another example of poetic engagement with the world, particularly the Israeli world, Darwish's poem "Identity Card" also written in 1964, brought forth the social determination of language that stresses the tensions within poetry as it consciously articulates the contradictions of the social world. Here, although not in a superb poetic form, Darwish's communicative capacity to create and to intervene with relative poetic prowess is demonstrated so as to render Palestinian situations and histories meaningful with great stressors placed on textual signification:

> Write down:
> a name with no friendly shortcut.
> A patient man, in a country
> brimming with anger.
> My roots have gripped this soil
> since time began,
> before the opening of ages
> before the cypress and the olive,
> before the grasses flourished.
> My father came from a line of
>   plowmen,
> And my grandfather was a peasant
> Who taught me about the sun's glory
> Before teaching me to read.
> My home is a watchman's shack
> Made of reeds and sticks
> Does my condition anger you?
> (1992: 214)

Whether Darwish was consciously portraying the real, that is the non-fictive, for affect, or simply was self-conscious of the poetics of poetry to the point of being pragmatic, is not at all an issue; Darwish's verses, ornamented or not, were conversing with history through the "I" and were already in connection with the "we". The objective as well as the symbolic "we" was the family, the land, and the occupied Palestinians. Thus, the real in Darwish's poetics was not an abstraction of the fictive, and what perhaps was fictive is an abstraction of the real that has hunted his creative landscape; the true space from which he was free to write and to be without being a "non-being" in a state of siege, or exile. Hence, my complete agreement with Wellek and Warren's affirmation on of the fusion between material world and language:

> In a successful work of art, the materials are completely assimilated into the form: what was 'world' has become 'language'. The 'materials' of a literary work of art are, on one level, words, on another level, human behaviour experience, and on another, human ideas and attitude. All of these, including language, exist outside the work of art, in other modes; but in a successful poem or novel they are pulled into polyphonic relations by the dynamic of aesthetic purpose. (Wellek & Warren, 1984: 241)

To critically read Darwish's text, one must construct relations between texts and world as well as with extratextual relationships that would inform the writer's intention and attitude. Again, aware of the weight of the word, Darwish's "Identity Card" is a poem that presupposes the reader's attitude by reading the reader and thus pre-imposing its meaning which the author prejudices by known discoveries, attitudes and articulations of expectations. This particular poem is drawn within the immediacy of the poetic space that reflects on itself while it simultaneously projects the reader's expected attitude within the textual field and the social operative field. In a sense, that particular poem was consciously constructed to be confrontational and ex-

pected responses that are a result of the interrogations that conclude each declarative stanza. "It's a poem that actually derives from the personal experience of having to register at an Israeli office" (Said, 2003: 161).

The poetic reflective tenacity of Darwish's discourse can be viewed through the production and consumption of his work as the inspiring mirror of the Palestinians and the Arab world. The reflective dimension of his work became apparent when he was popularly crowned as "the poet laureate of the Middle-East," a title he rejected because it was officious and not official. Nevertheless, the prowess of his works are reflected through the predominance of the poet's presence upon the cultural landscape as he voiced the pain, love, aspirations and simply the lyrical precision of words through the Arabic language that reflects and maintains its poetic eloquence present in progressive Islamic discourse. Edward Said also provides an accurate assessment of Darwish's poetic caliber as "a poet of many dimensions." "He's certainly a public poet, but also an intensely personal and lyrical poet. And I think, on the world scale today, he's certainly one of the best. He ranks with Derek Walcott and Seamus Heaney to mention two Nobel Prize winners, one from the Caribbean, one from Ireland in mastery of his language" (162). In a sense, through the mastery of the language, the poetic consciousness of the Arab further solidifies the bond felt through Darwish's poetics—hence, his essentialism as a modern poet who has flipped the categorization of Palestinians on its head and entered into a pseudo-direct dialogue with the Israeli occupier about the presence of life, love, liberty and memories of oppression, and includes the concentration camps in which the Jews died. In the formative period of Darwish's work, what is called for is to establish an understanding of a fully literary anthropological context of textual productions that occur within a tense social modality mandating implicit responses. The texts produced between 1964 and 1970, and even through the '70s, were indicative of the transgressed needs, as well as the personal age of radical militancy that rightly opposed a dehumanizing occupation. "It goes back to the Mahmoud Darwish poem about the identity card. Many Palestinians' identity cards don't list 'Palestinian' as one's nationality; they list one's nationality as 'undetermined'" (2003: 161). Thus, not only a trenchant voice arose and produced "Identity Card," "To The Reader," "Of Poetry," "Earth Poem," and "Prison"; but also, the poems composed in that period provided the literary anthropology to which I can assign a category, the Formative Period, that seems very distinctive in voice, outlook and *deontic* modality from the other two discerned categories. However, what remains constant throughout Mahmoud Darwish's poems and prose is that poetry is intrinsically connected to self-realization, and self-realization is a gradual, constantly dynamic and fluid process that is imbrued in his poetic project.

The ontological imposition of what a Palestinian is within the occupier's discourse was explicitly seized by Darwish's poem "Identity Card" and was re-imagined and re-ontologized in order to re-indicate the material condition of the Palestinians as an occupied people… Having outlined and hurled into the world the Palestinian as a conscious subject of the Israeli, and still being imbued with full memories of his past, Darwish's poem became the catalyst for his essential presence within the discursive framework of Palestinian identity and desire for independence from state-sponsored terror and occupation. "Identity Card" catapulted Darwish center stage to poetically counteract with the occupier.

III. SUBLIME: LOVE & EXILE

When Darwish's material Palestinian world is approximatively reduced to one of oppression and repression, it becomes fun-

damentally clear that in order to protect his psyche from becoming oppressed, his imaginative mind must turn to creativity, and thus finds a release center, compensation if you will. It is not that Darwish's works have changed the material world for Palestinians, but rather that his creative self has provided a psychical compensation that alleviates the pain from the actual conditions of repression. Love and hope become far greater weapons of resistance that do not allow the psyche to be broken.

The imaginative content of Darwish's love poems provides both emotional and ideological expressions that are overtly female and optimistic. It is precisely this use of writing style that makes Mahmoud Darwish such a respected and mesmeric writer. Even when writing about love, Darwish's writing was never demoted or démodé, nor robbed of its social and historical contexts, for exile was always there, never cut off from its socio-cultural lifeline:

I do not know why, I am so widely read, but I find there are generations of Palestinians who become acquainted with their homeland and their past by embodying the scenes of my poems. My poems do not deliver mere images and metaphors but deliver landscapes, villages, and fields, deliver a place. It makes that which is absent from geography present in its form, that is, able to reside the poetic text, as if residing on his land. I don't think that a poet is entitled to a greater happiness than that some people seek refuge in his lines of poetry, as if they were real houses. Indeed, in Arabic, there is a nice and unusual homonymy. Both the poetic verse and the house are said 'bayt'. As if a man can reside there. (Darwish, 1997: Documentary)

Since the self occupies multiple spaces

and is also fluid through its materialization and adaptation processes, one would be foolish to box Darwish, or other poets whose works are committed to witnessing, to a specific non-interactive category or categories, space, or creative voice. Again, Subbi Hadidi reminds us that Darwish's love poems "allow greater individual freedom and offer a spontaneous expression of profound emotions. Darwish's love poetry thus possesses a psychological infrastructure. This organizational method is certainly relevant to Darwish, his poetry, and his readers. Indeed, the structure negotiates the limits of the reader's interpretations of the poems as well as the emancipation of the poet's and reader's subjectivities" (111).

Darwish's textual communicative prowess can be measured through the interception, interpretation and renditions of his work through the Palestinian culture. Hence, his capacity to create and to imaginatively intervene in the routine of the people is indeed a rendering of their human lives meaningful through literature, despite an inhumane existence outside of the poetic text. As such, Darwish's language carried the weight of his historicity within his literary monde that encountered prison, exile, love, hope, despair, return and occupation. His poems on love and exile are maps of his diasporic journeys. Beyond the aesthetically pleasing poetic construction of the love poems, there are the incidences of dislocation, displacement, and dashed hopes. The archaeology of those particular poems is therefore an extended meditative container for dislocation, unsustainable love due to flight, unanchored diasporic lives, and the pain involved in experiencing brutal repression while maintaining hope in the face of a dwindling *self-ruled cage* that might become the eventual Palestinian homeland:

Two of my verses, which have become popular, seem to contradict each other, although, in my opinion, they are complimentary. The

first, which has become something of a motto, is 'my homeland is not a suitcase, and I am not a traveler.' Years later, this suitcase spoke with itself and said, 'my homeland is a suitcase.' I see no contradiction between the two statements. When I examine how I feel as an exile, I find that my exile did not begin outside my homeland but inside it. The military Judge who punish[ed] me for my poetry was Jewish. The woman teacher who taught me Hebrew and inspired my love for literature, was Jewish. The English teacher, a stern man, was Jewish. The woman Judge who presided over my first trial was Jewish. My first lover was Jewish, my next door neighbor was Jewish, and my political comrades were Jewish. Therefore, I did not look at Jews as a separate entity; I did not have a stereotypes view. Thus from the beginning for me, coexistence has seemed possible psychologically and culturally, but the main problem remains the political one. (Darwish, 1997: Documentary)

Love and Exile are firmly established themes throughout Darwish's work. They form a complex anthropological map, of contentious spaces and perspectives. The poem "She's Alone in the Evening" captures this form of poetic anthropological mapping where desire and loneliness form the master narrative of the poem, and where the subtext remains the plight of exile and a language that is silenced:

She's alone, and I am in front of beauty
Alone. Why doesn't delicacy unite us?
I say to myself
Why don't I taste her wine?
She doesn't see me, when I see her
uncrossing her legs…
And I also don't see her, when she sees

me
taking off my coat…
Nothing bothers her when she's with
    me
nothing bothers me, because we are
    now
harmonious in forgetfulness…
Our dinner was, separately, delicious
the night sound was blue
I wasn't alone, and neither was she
    alone
we were together listening to the
    crystal
(nothing fractures our night). (2007: 265)

Love is the space within which a continuous process of self—of emotional evolution—takes place in order to reach humanity's apex, and exile is the space of longing for what is imaginatively desirable or at least a return to the known and the familiar. In a re-rooting of the self, those two spaces create a hyperspace of desire and longing where the self binds to its primal relationship, its receptacle nature, the native land. As Ibtisam Barakat accurately expressed, and I will hitch my thoughts with hers "Who in the world would not be able to relate to missing their mother! Words that symbolized the state of exile for the Palestinians in the most universal of words…but also could reach the farthest points of the human heart…" (2008: Roundtable).

The Reading of Darwish's poetic corpus as literary anthropology is further supported by the poet's statement as quoted by Subbi Hadidi:

>…Regarding poetic language, poetry is in a general way a journey between cultures, languages, and different temporalities. Poetry cannot be nationalist in the strict meaning of the word; but, because of the fact that there is a link between poetry and community and because the poet belongs in some way to this community and is the product of a particular historic configuration, has a role in shaping the cultural identity of his people. (2008: 108)

Darwish's conscious reading and interpretation of his role as poet solidifies my argument that his aesthetic and poetic project is not simply literary, but firmly cultural with a philosophical appendage reminiscent of the ancient Greeks. He acts a poet-philosopher whose task is to represent and meet the need of the collective and yet inspire them. Thus, the existence of a co-mingling between the private and the public, freedom and un-freedom, and the overall desire for the poet to please himself is but to be embraced by his readers. Hence the importance of his expressed sentiment in Simone Bitton's 1997 documentary:

>The harmony of poetry, the rhythm of poetry cannot be realized unless a lyrical atmosphere pervades the poem. An atmosphere which requires certain harmonic and rhythmic conditions not found in poems written in private. I write a poem in private, but transmitted to the people, it becomes a different poem, dissociated from the written text. It creates another ritual, a celebration between the image, the voice, the body and the collective rewriting of the text.

Through the cinematograhic lens of the documentary "Mahmoud Darwish as Land is Language," a Film by Simone Bitton (France 3/ PDJ Productions: 1997), I was able to further comprehend and solidify my interpretation of Darwish's works. While on Mount Nebo in Jordan, Darwish looked out on the Eastern Slope of the Dead Sea to contemplate his homeland cradling just beyond the River Jordan, and said: "The dialogue I conduct with myself here, is a dialogue with the absent part of me. I see absence so closely that I can touch it. I can embrace it, or keep it away, as if I were there. As if my shadow here addresses my essence there." Haunted by the absence of the sacred, one's birthplace, Darwish's poems hunts the imagination of the reader for his lyricism and his imageries are agencies that elicit compassion. The poem "Who Am I, Without Exile" captures that essence:

> Water
> binds me
> to your name…
> There's nothing left of me but you, and
>   nothing left of you
> but me, the stranger massaging his
>   stranger's thigh: O
> stranger! What will we do with what is
>   left to us
> of calm… and of a snooze between two
>   myths?
> And nothing carries us: not the road
>   and not the house.
> Was this road always like this, from the
>   start,
> or did our dreams find a mare on the
>   hill
> among the Mongol horses and
>   exchange us for it?
> And what will we do?
> What
> will we do
> without
> exile? (2007: 89)

The existential questions along with the problems faced by the strangers in the poem create a psychic doubling that requires a split consciousness in order to deal with the ordeal of natal-landlessness and the intense love for a shattered and occupied land. And where, as a result of dislocation, one's love cannot be grounded due to constant movement and unwanted fragmentation that forced exile engenders:

> I feel somewhat like a stranger.
> One may feel a stranger even in the

mirror. There is something missing, and that is what pains me most. I feel that I am like a tourist but without the rights of a tourist. This feeling of being a visitor is devastating. The most difficult thing is to be a visitor to oneself… A Palestinian cannot reach Jerusalem. I myself cannot reach Jerusalem. I myself cannot hold that full moon. All I can do is to bear my disappointment and return to the cage to which I am doomed. (Darwish, 1997: Documentary)

In the Sublime period of Darwish's work, love becomes the nursing ground for imaginative poetic maturation as well as the house that nurtures the fragmented exiled-self. Again, an understanding must be established of the literary anthropological context of Darwish's textual productions that occurred within a tense period of rupture and flight. The texts produced between 1982-1995 were indicative of the imaginative and personal freedom needs that sublimely counteracted with his dehumanizing existence as a landless exile.

Through being incognito in Paris, although coincidental, Darwish benefited from isolation by becoming much more prolific and delved into his own psychological terrain, his geography of exile and longing, and therefore composed his best work. Here, he addressed the hardship of dislocation and defeat as a stateless being, as well as the carnal desire of the poet. "Of course, I have longings and inner drives, and there is a stirring in the blood, calling for the other, but not in any institutional sense" (1997, Documentary). As for carnal desire, in a passage from "Memory for Forgetfulness" he writes in a somewhat journalistic prose: "I turn to the poet: 'Tell me, why do young men get excited under the worst conditions? Is this a time for love? This is no time for love, but for sudden desire. Two fleeting bodies collaborate to hold back one fleeting death by means of another—a hon-eyed death'" (1995: 57). Although tragic, the Palestinian's existentiality or will to ex-ist despite the certainty of death, embraces the affirmation of life through the human embrace as a primordial human condition, albeit carnal desire.

The creative freedom achieved in Paris temporarily liberated Darwish's trauma-tized-exiled psyche and delved into cre-ation. It was because of Paris, after being bestowed as a Knight of Arts and Belles Lettres, that he achieved international rec-ognition and his work began to be widely translated. Thus he expanded the geo-graphical recognition of Palestine and the Palestinian plight with a dashing hope of a possibility of a right to return. The univer-sality of his work, whether longing for the homeland, longing for love, or expressing the horror of living under occupation, brought the voice and the ordeal of the mar-ginalized to the center:

> Perhaps one of the reasons why I like Paris is that I don't speak French, which kept me on the mar-gin of French life, without mixing with the neighbors or society in general. This gave me greater free-dom to be what I want to be and to act as I want. When I walk in the streets, nobody knows me. In an Arab country, I cannot sit alone in a café, for there, people recognize me and come to greet me. I cannot read my newspaper nor meditate. Here, I am an unknown person. Here, I wrote my best works: 'It is a Song, It is a Song'; 'Fewer Roses'; 'I See What I Want'; 'Eleven Stars'. The last work I wrote here was 'Why You Left Me Alone?' In addi-tion, I wrote some prose works: 'A Memory For Forgetfulness'; and 'Passers among Passing Words'. (Darwish, 1997: Documentary)

The Sublime stage is indicative of the creative dissident imagination that sus-tained Darwish's humanity and bestowed the freedom to push his fierce modernist creativity while maintaining a literary link with the classical past. His creative dissi-dent imagination allowed him to rebel-liously innovate without alienating himself and his readers. Through his innovative realms, history is still center stage.

IV. GLOBAL: HUMANITY, RETURN, DASHED HOPE

The global has become a metaphor from which I am able to further theorize on the last decade of Darwish's work. The post-trenchant (Formative) period is where the self is solely centered upon the national. The gaze of the trenchant is immediate and my-opically precise, and thus, the immediate must be understood, explicated and voiced. Anger, shame and humiliation embodies the trenchant and the response is always *du tac au tac*. That is, the global becomes bi-fo-cal and pluralistic in tone while the content is still singular and contains a Palestinian consciousness. The singularity of the "I" becomes the universal, the "I" can be inhab-ited by the reader, as if in an echo chamber or a mirror effect had occurred. The last nineteen lines from the poem "Cadence Chooses Me" perfectly illustrate this point:

> …
> Whenever I listen to the stone I hear
> the cooing of a white pigeon
> gasp in me:
> My brother! I am your little sister,
> So I cry in her name the tears of speech
> And whenever I see the zanzalakht
>   trunk
> on the way to the clouds,
> I hear a mother's heart
> palpitate in me:
> I am a divorced woman,
> so I curse in her name the cicada
>   darkness

And whenever I see a mirror on a moon
I see love a devil
glaring at me:
I am still here
but you won't return as you were when
    I left you
you won't return, and I won't return
Then cadence completes its cycle
and chokes on me... (2007: 179)

The global, although it is still national, is in a non-contradictory co-existence with the universal. That is, Darwish's connectivity with the world was never a negation of the local, instead, it intensified the connection with the locale but with an ontology and epistemology that could be grasped by the "we" of the global, particularly the struggling global.

The witnessing poet relocates occupational practices from the hidden to the open and declaratively categorizes the events in terms of human occurrences and refuses margins in order to be "read" as center, as anthropological events and not simply as raw historical events. The poet puts a face, a content, behind the number of person "X" whose house was bulldozed, whose olive groves were destroyed and whose land was seized. The poet writes with an intimate intentionality, with a conscious articulation about social & personal events that have personified contours and historical data. In fact, for Darwish, historical writing is the antithesis of poetry. Thus in the prose-poem "Don't Write History as Poetry" this is his fundamental plea:

Don't write poetry as history, because
    the weapon is
the historian. And the historian
    doesn't get fever
chills when names his victims, and
    doesn't listen
to the guitar's rendition. And history is
    the dailiness
of weapons prescribed upon our
    bodies. [...]

Aimlessly we make it and it make us...
    Perhaps
history wasn't born as we desired,
    because
the Human Being never existed?
Philosophers and artists passed
    through there...
and the poets wrote down the dailiness
    of their purple flowers
then passed through there... and the
    poor believed
in sayings about paradise and waited
    there...
and gods came to rescue nature from
    our divinity
and passed through there. And history
    has no
time for contemplation, history has no
    mirror
and bare face. It is unreal reality
or unfanciful fancy, so don't write it.
Don't write it, don't write it as poetry!
    (2007: 259)

During an interview with Sarah Adler, an Israeli television reporter, Darwish was asked to clarify his view on his usage of Homer as it relates to Israel and the Israelis' rights to the land. And he provided an answer that elucidated his poetic project and his complex understanding of the poetic of politics:Darwish's poetic corpus can be viewed as a discourse that articulates a Palestinian consciousness of history and a social project for the region that is based on respect for humanity and self. It is a consciousness that is linked to and dependent upon the fate of the nation within which all hopes are located. Darwish's poetic discourse situates him within a global context where dichotomous visions of nation-states are expressed in a supposed postcolonial framework, but where coloniality within the Israeli-Palestinian conflict is at the center of history.

Truth has two faces. We've listened
to the Greek mythology and, at

times, we've heard the Trojan victim speak through the myth of the Greek Euripides. As for me, I'm looking for the poet of Troy, because Troy didn't tell its story. And I wonder, does a land that has great poets have the right to control a people that have no poets? And is the lack of poetry amongst a people enough reason to justify its defeat? Is poetry a sign or is it an instrument of power? Can a people be strong without having its own poetry?

I was a child of people that had not been recognized until then. And I wanted to speak in the name of the absentee in the name of Trojan poet. There's more inspiration and humanity in defeat than there is in victory.

[**Sarah**: 'Are you sure?']...

In defeat, there's also deep romanticism in defeat. If I belonged to the victor's camp, I'd demonstrate my support for the victims. Do you know why the Palestinians are famous? Because you are our enemy. The interest in us stems from the interest in the Jewish issue. The interest is in you, not in me. So, we have the misfortune of having Israel as an enemy because it enjoys unlimited support. And we have the great fortune of having Israel as our enemy because the Jews are the center of attention. You've brought us defeat and renown. You've brought us defeat and renown...

[**Sarah**: 'We are your propaganda Ministry!']

Indeed. The world is interested in you, not us. I have no illusions.[1]

It is within such scope and complex outlook that Darwish's writing really fused and incorporated well-known mythologies into his writing in order to elucidate his points. That the Palestinian struggle was no longer a solitary struggle for a small group of people, but a struggle of the world, and also a struggle that belonged to the Israelis whose humanity he recognized was afflicted by the dehumanizing acts they inflicted upon the Palestinians.

In a sense, exile and suffering enabled Darwish to transcend the confines of nationalistic borders without losing his national identity, while becoming transnational as a grounded Palestinian poet with an "autonomous" identity that enabled him to simultaneously reflect inward and outward. The globalizing essence of his later writings unbounded his occupied identity, and essentialized his Palestinian self that was restricted in a context of inhumane occupation. Through his works, we, the non-Palestinans, became Palestinians and lament and hope with him for a new dawn; but the harsh reality of the occupation, despite his creative dissidence of the imagination, ushers in a cruel reality that even the most resilient poet must admit:

> I consider myself a Trojan poet, that poet whose text has been lost to us and literary history. What I wish to express, although not with any finality, but with a certain ambiguity, is that I belong to Troy, not because I am defeated, but because I am obsessed by the desire to write the lost text. Of course, I would rather be victorious in the general sense, that is to say, not to belong to a defeated society, in order to test the validity of my desire to embody the sacrificed Troy, which can then write its own history... ...I

---

[1] http://www.dailymotion.com/playlist/ x61vo_lapierreetlaplume_soustitres-fr/video/ x3mr07_mahmoud-darwich-sarah-adler

have a problem I would like to confess. I have not yet acknowledged that I am defeated. It may be that the illusion of creating has provided me with weapons that protect me from seeing the extent of the effect of the military and political defeat. Maybe I refuse to see it. Maybe a defeat is not ineluctable at the creative and poetic level. (Darwish, 1997: Documentary)

The philosopher-poet, or poet-philosopher, who had been exiled since the age of six, carried memories with him in his poetic suitcase from port to port and never fully grounded in one place. Even to visit his family in Israel, he had received a restricted state permit that allowed him, in 1997, for five days to be with his extended family, including his mother. His last and brief visit to Israel occurred on July 15, 2007, to attend a poetry recital. The poet-philosopher who is de-rooted from the familial found solace in poetry and conveys to the world his knowledge, his historicity, in a non-historical way. His daily contemplations become "ours" and we lament, laugh and hope with the poet because his voice forms symbiotic relations with ours as he resides inside of us with a poetic certainty and familiarity.

As a Non-Palestinian, and Non-Arab, but as a human being and a poet, I too mourned the passing of an elder poet. Darwish was a poet-philosopher, a national Palestinian poet, who died in August 9, 2008, in Houston, Texas as a result of heart failure at only 67 years old. Following the tradition of respect for the elder, as Khalis and Rahman did in their edited collection on Darwish, I too will give him the last word:

As the collective is closer to achieving its project, as the *nashid* becomes less serious, arrival is the last stanza. And when arrival has been achieved and identity with it, then beauty allows for an individu-

al voice. So the repressed within the individual has an opening and a possibility for expression. The Palestinian question has not been resolved, but it has been transformed from its human dimension to its administrative dimension. We are not present and we are not absent. But we are linked to the idea of a state. (Darwish, 2008: 324)

REFERENCES

Adler, Sarah. "Mahmoud Darwish & Sarah Adler." http://www.dailymotion.com/playlist/x61vo_lapierreetlaplume_soustitres-fr/video/x3mr07_mahmoud-darwich-sarah-adler

Asfour, John Mikhail. *When the Words Burn*: An *Anthology of Modern Arabic Poetry, 1945-1987*. Egypt: The American University in Cairo Press. 1992.

Barakat, Ibtisam. "Roundtable on Mahmoud Darwish". Discussion/Interview. *IMEU*, Sep 12, 2008. http://imeu.net/news/article0014104.shtml

Bitton, Simone. "Mahmoud Darwish as Land is Language." Documentary Film. France 3/ PDJ Productions: 1997

Brink, André. "The Writer as Witch." *The Dissident Word: Oxford Amnesty Lectures, 1995*. Ed. Chris Miller. New York: Basic Books.1996.

Césaire, Aimé. *Lyric and Dramatic Poetry: 1946-82*. Charlottes: University Press of Virginia. 1990.

Darwish, Mahmoud. *The Butterfly's Burden*. Washington: Copper Canyon Press. 2007.

Darwish, Mahmoud. *Memory For Forgetfulness: August, Beirut, 1982*. Berkley: University of California Press. 1995.

Darwish, Mahmoud. *Victims of a Map: A Bilingual Anthology of Arabic Poetry*. London: SAQI Books. 1995.

Forché, Carolyn. *Against Forgetting: Twentieth Century Poetry of witness*. New York: W. W. Norton & Co. 1993.

Hadidi, Subbi. "Mahmoud Darwish's Love Poem: History, Exile, and the Epic Call." *Mahmoud Darwish: Exile's Poet*. Ed. Hala Khamis & Najat Rahman. Massachusetts: Olive Branch Press. 2008.

Miller, Chris. "Introduction." *The Dissident Word: Oxford Amnesty Lectures, 1995*. Ed. Chris Miller. New York: Basic Books.1996.

Rahman, Najat. "Interview with Mahmoud Darwish: On the Possibility Poetry at a Time of Siege." *Mahmoud Darwish: Exile's Poet*. Ed. Hala Khamis & Najat Rahman. Massachusetts: Olive Branch Press. 2008.

Said, Edward W. *Culture and Resistance: conversations with Edward W. Said /David Barsamian*. Cambridge, MA: South End Press. 2003.

Wellek, René & Warren, Austin. *Theory of Literature*. Third Edition. New York: Harcourt Brace & Co. 1956.

CPSIA information can be obtained
at www.ICGtesting.com
Printed in the USA
LVHW061251140323
741536LV00034B/2363

9 781888 024364